Dyslexia: An Irish Perspective

About the Authors

Mary Ball is a psychologist working with the Dyslexia Association of Ireland. Before training as a psychologist she taught for many years, at secondary level and was involved with adult education. For a number of years she delivered the courses in educational psychology to trainee teachers in the National College of Art. She has given courses to learning support teachers and special needs assistants on dyslexia and is a contributor to the Dyslexia Association Parents' Course. Her work with the Dyslexia Association includes assessing children and adults with reading difficulties, and supporting and directing the educational work of the Association.

Anne Hughes is the Director of the Dyslexia Association of Ireland. A social worker by profession, she joined the DAI when her son was diagnosed with dyslexia. She began work with the association in l985. Over the past 20 years she has worked with parents, teachers, adults with dyslexia and local groups to promote awareness of dyslexia and to lobby for better services. She set up the only full-time course in Ireland for adults with dyslexia in l998. She has been a guest speaker at conferences in the UK, Norway and Sweden. She carries out disability awareness training and speaks to parents and community groups on dyslexia.

Wyn McCormack is a guidance counsellor and resource teacher at St. David's School, Greystones and is also the parent of sons who have dyslexia. She is a long term member of the Dyslexia Association of Ireland and has served on its National Executive for several years. She is the author of the book *Lost for Words – a practical guide to dyslexia at second level* which was published in 1998 and reprinted in 2002. She has given talks to groups of parents and teachers and provided in-service training on the topic to dyslexia to second level schools and teachers. She has campaigned for the development of support structures in schools for students with dyslexia and is a strong advocate for equity in the Irish education system, which should allow students with dyslexia participate on an equal basis with other students.

Dyslexia:
An Irish Perspective

M. BALL, A. HUGHES AND W. MCCORMACK

BLACKHALL
Publishing

This book was typeset by Folio Publishing Services for

Blackhall Publishing
33 Carysfort Avenue
Blackrock
Co. Dublin
Ireland

Email: info@blackhallpublishing.com
www.blackhallpublishing.com

© Ball, Hughes and McCormack, 2006

ISBN: 1 842180 95 9

A catalogue record for this book is available from the
British Library.

Printed in Ireland by
ColourBooks Ltd

Contents

Acknowledgements

The authors would like to thank the Dyslexia Association of Ireland for support and encouragement in the writing of this book. We would also like to pay tribute to all the people with dyslexia whom we have met and worked with over the years. The effort and determination shown by these children and adults to overcome their dyslexia has been an inspiration. Particular mention should be made of Robin, Simon and Daragh, without whom two of us would never have gotten involved in campaigning on behalf of people with dyslexia.

Many thanks are due to Rosie Bissett for her painstaking reading of the manuscript. Her meticulous editing and insightful comments were invaluable.

Finally, we would like to thank and to acknowledge the professionalism of Blackhall Publishing. This book arose from an initiative by Ailbhe O'Reilly and Ruth Garvey. We are indebted to both for their encouragement and advice. We would also like to thank Gerard O'Connor and Mariel Deegan who saw the project through to completion. The delightful book cover is the work of designer, Susan Waine. To one and all, our grateful thanks.

Foreword

Somerset Maugham (I think) wrote a short story about a sexton in a small parish church who was extremely good at his job. The job was humble, the pay modest, but he was driven by a strong sense of commitment to his work, a sense that he was an important part of his local community. He took great pride in ensuring that the church was always clean, that the flowers were fresh, and that the boiler was always properly stoked. As a consequence, the church was always a warm and welcoming place.

All was well until a new curate was appointed to the parish. In his very first interview with the sexton, he discovered that this faithful servant of the church could neither read nor write. Thinking himself to be a highly progressive sort, the curate explained to the sexton that it would be impossible for him to undertake the new range of tasks he had in mind, such as maintaining the register of births and marriages, because of this defect. In vain the sexton protested that there was nothing that had prevented him from carrying out his duties to the highest possible standard. No, the curate insisted, he was sorry, but there would have to be a parting of the ways. A new sexton, with all the skills necessary, would have to be appointed. And in the wink of an eye, the sexton found himself out of a job.

Normally he took the long walk home in his stride. This evening, though, he felt a weariness in his step, and his journey through the town's main street seemed awfully long. Seeking comfort in a pipe of tobacco, he was even more upset to discover that his tobacco pouch was empty – and that there was nowhere, all along the length of the main street, where he could buy an ounce of his favourite tobacco to replenish it.

Sitting at home that night, he had an idea. Although he now had no job, he had accumulated some modest savings – enough, he discovered, to rent a small vacant store on the main street. Soon he had opened the town's first dedicated tobacconist shop, and with the skills he had applied to his previous job, he had made it into a warm and welcoming haven.

Within two years, he had seven shops, one in each of the towns and villages around. His thriving business soon caught the eye of a larger corporation, whose general manager was very impressed by the intimacy of these shops and the standards of quality and service their proprietor had insisted on. Seeking him out, the business magnate made the former sexton a handsome offer for the shops, more than enough to guarantee a happy and comfortable retirement.

Once the offer was accepted, the moment came for the handing over of a large cheque and the signing of the contract. It was then that the businessman discovered that the former sexton could neither read nor write.

"Good lord," said the businessman. "With your talent and business acumen, heaven only knows what you would be if you could read and write."

The former sexton could only smile wryly. If he could read and write, he would still be a humble sexton.

Or maybe it could be put another way. If he hadn't been discriminated against in the first place, he might never have discovered his true calling. The discovery that he was unable to read and write led to assumptions being made about him that simply weren't true. I don't know if that sexton had dyslexia, but I do know that dyslexia is not, in itself, a barrier to achievement that cannot be overcome. The insurmountable barriers are all created by assumptions and attitudes.

I don't have dyslexia, though I have friends who do. Through other circumstances, I have some experience of what it feels like to be treated as a second-class citizen, and I know that some of my friends have felt stigmatised by their dyslexia. But they are talented, intelligent, social and creative people, who know that life places hurdles in everyone's way. The tragedy is when the hurdles are built up higher by ignorance, misunderstanding and sometimes sheer intolerance. And it happens.

The result is that for a great many individuals and families, the circumstances surrounding dyslexia amount to a sense of stigmatisation. The purpose of this book, at least in part, is to end the stigma, and place dyslexia in its proper perspective.

On average, at least ten members of Dáil Eireann have dyslexia. Of all the people who have served in Government over the last fifteen years or so, at least two or three have had dyslexia. Dyslexia exists in the upper reaches of the civil service, in the boardrooms of our major corporations, among leading sportspeople, musicians and artists. All had, and have, a disability. Some got the appropriate level of assessment and support. Others did not.

There are keys to overcoming any disability, to tearing down the barriers. The first is early assessment. The second is suitable and appropriate support. And the third is openness. There is no reason whatever why dyslexia should be a subject people are afraid to discuss, because the more we know, the less reason there is for misunderstanding and fear.

I hope this book helps to put the subject of dyslexia on the agenda. As well as being a practical guide, it helps to dispel the myths and to create a proper sense of dyslexia as one more of life's hurdles – and a hurdle that can be overcome.

1. Introduction

Charlemagne, the most powerful of the Holy Roman Emperors, was dyslexic. How do we know? Well, we don't really, but look at the evidence. Charlemagne was a very clever man. He was a brilliant administrator, an enlightened leader and a great scholar. He loved learning and founded schools, monasteries and even universities. He studied *furiously* according to one biographer but could never master Latin or Greek. All through his life he tried to learn to write. He even kept writing tablets by his bed so that he could practise but he never succeeded. Could his difficulties have been caused by his ninth century schooling? This is unlikely because he brought the best teachers of the age to his court; his wife and daughters, who studied with him, appeared to have no such problems.

So did Charlemagne have dyslexia? If he did, and all the signs are there, then this would indicate that dyslexia is nothing new. Indeed, when reading about historical figures, it is surprising how often learning difficulties are described. From King Louis XV of France to Thomas Edison, from William Butler Yeats to Winston Churchill, the childhood and educational experiences of many famous and successful people show evidence of what might now be diagnosed as dyslexia. But the word dyslexia was not used then because the condition did not become widely known until the mid-twentieth century. This has led some commentators to suggest that dyslexia is a modern invention and almost by implication to suggest that it is a vogue rather than an actual condition. This view has caused a great deal of distress to people with dyslexia and has allowed many of those who ought to know better not to take dyslexia seriously.

Fortunately, scientific research has provided evidence that dyslexia is a neurological condition that most certainly affects the lives of many people. Educationalists now agree that dyslexia is indeed a fact; while there is still some argument about the prevalence of the difficulty, nobody seriously questions its existence. Research from English-speaking countries would indicate that 6 to 8 per cent of the population is affected by dyslexia to some extent. Some professionals put the figure at 10 per cent. This means that, in a class of thirty students, there could be three pupils with some form of dyslexia. These statistics highlight the challenge dyslexia poses to our education system.

In Ireland, the Department of Education and Science recognises that children with dyslexia have distinct educational needs. Support for children with specific learning disabilities has been in place since 1975 but it is only within the last decade that substantial developments have taken place. These include:

- The Report of the Task Force on Dyslexia published by the Department of Education and Science in 2001. This was followed a year later by a similar Task Force Report in Northern Ireland. Both reports adopt the same comprehensive definition of dyslexia. The report published by the Irish Department of Education and Science described the existing provision and made 61 recommendations. There has been progress on some of these recommendations since then.
- Recommendation One of the Report was that information and advice should be readily available to teachers and parents/ guardians of children with dyslexia through the development of printed and electronic material for distribution through the schools. This resulted in the publication in 2005 of the video/CD ROM/DVD *Understanding Dyslexia*. This excellent and comprehensive package has been distributed to all primary and post-primary schools. It is also available from Government Publications at the price of €10.
- The Education Act 1998 made provision for equality of access to and participation in Irish schools for students and that schools should provide appropriate education for pupils, taking into account the child's abilities and needs.
- The Education of Persons with Special Educational Needs Act 2004 provided the right for inclusive education within mainstream schools for the child with special educational needs. Special educational needs are defined in the Act as:

> A restriction in the capacity of the person to participate in and benefit from education on account of an enduring physical, sensory, mental health or learning disability, or any other condition which results in a person learning differently from a person without that condition.

This definition means that children with dyslexia are covered under this Act and so have certain rights and entitlements, which are set out in sections two to eighteen of the Act. Children with special educational needs should have an individual education plan (IEP). Parents have the right to be involved when the IEP is being drawn up.

- The Learning Support Guidelines were published by the Department of Education and Science in 2000. These Guidelines provide practical guidance to teachers and to parents on the provision of effective learning support to pupils with low achievement/learning difficulties. The Guidelines recommend that an individual profile and learning programme (IPLP) should be drawn up and parents should be involved in the planning of this document.
- The establishment of the National Educational Psychological Service (NEPS).
- The establishment of the Special Education Support Service (SESS), which provides training on the topic of special needs for teachers at primary and post-primary levels. SESS has set up a team of teachers specialised in the topic of dyslexia with a view to providing training at primary and post-primary level.
- The development of supports for students in the state examinations and at third-level colleges.
- Increased numbers of special needs teachers.
- The improved understanding of dyslexia has led to more methods being developed to help these students learn. It has also enabled students to make more informed educational choices.
- Individuals with dyslexia benefit from the advances made in information and communications technology. Programmes such as voice-operated software, spelling and grammar checkers, predictive text programmes and scanners that read text aloud can be particularly helpful to students with dyslexia.
- A review of teacher training is planned. It is hoped that teachers in the future will have more expertise in the area of special educational needs and will receive training in the identification of learning difficulties.

While all of this is very welcome, there is much more that can be done. It would not be wise to assume that children with dyslexia will now have all their needs met within the official education system. There are grounds for concern for parents and teachers that gaps and anomalies remain. Some of these are:

- Absence of a continuum of provision. Support within the school system is provided, for the most part, to those students who experience the most severe difficulties. In theory, schools may allocate learning support where they see the need. In reality, time and resources are limited, so only those with the lowest reading and spelling attainments are targeted. This means that there are many children with dyslexia who are not achieving their full learning potential, but who are not perceived as in need of learning support. Because the difficulties experienced by students range from mild to severe, support should be available at a variety of levels, appropriate to the individual learning needs. This was a guiding principle of the work of the Task Force on Dyslexia which stated that:

> A continuum of support and services should be available to students with learning difficulties arising from dyslexia matched to the severity and persistence of their learning difficulties ... Programme planning and provision for students with learning difficulties arising from dyslexia should focus on individual learning needs.

Unfortunately, this is not yet the case. Indeed the increasing numbers of students identified with dyslexia has led to its being classified by the Department of Education and Science as a high incidence disability and students in this classification do not qualify for individual resource teaching at primary level, whatever the degree of their difficulty.

- Delays in the identification of dyslexic difficulties.
- Continuing difficulty in obtaining full psycho-educational assessment.
- A trend towards minimising the importance of psycho-educational assessment. This has been influenced by the change in policy whereby children may receive learning support without having a full assessment. It should be noted that there is no change in the requirement of full psycho-educational assessment in order to secure exemption from the study of Irish or admission to special reading schools or classes. Full assessment reports are requested by third-level colleges for students seeking support for dyslexia and such reports are also valuable when applying for special accommodation when sitting the Leaving Certificate examinations.
- The lack of knowledge about dyslexia amongst many teachers, particularly at second level.
- The small number of second-level teachers who attend in-service courses on dyslexia.
- The difficulties experienced by classroom and special needs teachers in preparing and implementing appropriate education plans for children with dyslexia.

- Limitation of support for second-level students with dyslexia.
- The nature and extent of reasonable accommodations in state examinations and the difficulty in accessing them.
- Presence of endorsements on certificates of students who receive accommodation in state exams.

There have been many changes in policy and administration within the Department of Education in recent years and it will take some time to establish just how these will affect the provision of services. In a fluid situation it is difficult to make an accurate assessment. Factors from budgetary constraints to the outcome of court cases, from prevailing educational theories to changes of personnel in crucial areas of government, all play a part in determining the provision of services. Public and particularly parental demand is hugely significant too, but parents are not always conscious of the difficulties that exist.

It is easy to see the flaws in the physical structures of schools. Dilapidated school buildings, leaky pre-fabricated classrooms or inadequate toilet facilities are very obvious and parents and teachers rightly campaign for their replacement. It is not as easy to see where the systemic difficulties lie. Unless a parent encounters a specific difficulty, the absence of the relevant service may never become apparent. Sometimes the gap in provision is only evident in retrospect. Sins of omission are less easy to detect than those of commission.

Perhaps the single most frequent omission cited by parents is the failure of school authorities to identify a dyslexic difficulty at an early stage. The reason for this is likely to be linked to the pre-service training that teachers receive. This does not always equip teachers to identify a dyslexic difficulty or to assess a child's learning needs adequately. The Report of the Task Force on Dyslexia strongly recommended in-service and in-career development courses for teachers, as well as more pre-service training in the area of dyslexia.

Ms Mary Hanafin, Minister for Education and Science, announced in May 2005 that a review of teacher training to keep pace with modern needs was planned. The Minister asked, 'How can we better equip mainstream class teachers with the training required for the early identification of learning difficulties and for assisting children with learning difficulties?' The Minister's question may have been prompted by the Task Force Report of 2000, but it could equally have been triggered by an evaluation by the Inspectorate of the Department of Education and Science into Literacy and Numeracy in Disadvantaged Schools, published in 2005. This report noted:

> The vast majority of teachers interviewed indicated that their initial teacher training did not prepare them sufficiently for the challenge of their present teaching situation and that their training was not an effective preparation for teaching in a disadvantaged setting. The teachers referred to their day-to-day practice in the schools as being very removed from theory addressed in colleges.

In relation to in-school assessment of the learning needs of children, the Inspectors reported:

> The provision of a coherent approach to the assessment and monitoring of children's progress was very weak and required significant development. The majority of teachers were rated as experiencing significant difficulty or requiring development in the area of organising assessment information about individual pupils.

The Inspectors also found that the group tests used did not give 'sufficient details of individual children's strengths and weaknesses'.

There is no reason to assume that these difficulties exist only in schools in disadvantaged areas. There appears to be a significant cause for parents of children with dyslexia to wonder if teachers are sufficiently informed to be able to detect the difficulty at an early stage, and whether the test procedures available within schools are sensitive enough to pinpoint the problem and thorough enough to inform appropriate interventions. The proposed review may yield changes in teacher training in the future. In the meantime parents have to be aware of any deficits that exist in the current system.

It is interesting to note that a survey of members of the Dyslexia Association of Ireland in 2000 found that parents were alerted to the existence of their child's problem by the school in 35 per cent of cases. Five years later, a survey of 40 second-level students with dyslexia found exactly the same percentage had their problem first identified by their school. This indicates either that school authorities were reluctant to mention the subject to parents or that the problem was not picked up by the school.

It is widely recognised that the earlier a dyslexic difficulty is recognised and appropriate support given, the better the chance that the child will cope effectively with the school curriculum. Delays in identification leave time for a culture of failure to set in, for damage to self-esteem and a distaste for school and learning to be acquired. Children whose difficulties are recognised and who get educational and emotional support can usually achieve their potential. They can grow up as happy human beings, coping with school, examinations and college or further training. Third-level institutions report ever-increasing numbers of such students at undergraduate and postgraduate levels. They are to be found in all occupations, trades, professions and amongst the self-employed and entrepreneurs. They are productive citizens who achieve in their chosen career, despite their learning difficulties.

Given the importance of early and adequate diagnosis of dyslexia, it is worrying that despite the establishment of a National Educational Psychological Service, parents and teachers still experience difficulties and delays in securing full psycho-educational assessment. There is a view in certain educational circles that parents request assessment too readily and the demand on scarce resources is not warranted. Psycho-educational assessment is a time-consuming and expensive procedure, but it is very important for children and adults with dyslexia. Learning support is available in schools without resort to full assessment. This gives much needed flexibility to schools and allows for the provision of learning support at an early stage. Assessment may not be necessary to avail of learning support within school but it may well be necessary for the subtler details of a child's difficulty to be pinpointed or to distinguish between general and specific learning difficulty. Preparation of a detailed individual pupil learning profile (IPLP), advice to parents in terms of expectations and levels of support, referral for additional medical or professional investigation, referral to special reading schools and applications for exemption from the study of Irish and exam accommodations all rely heavily on the expertise of the psychologist and the information provided in a professional assessment report.

While the numbers of special educational needs teachers at primary level is substantial, resources are only now being put in place at second level. Indeed, the impression could well be gained that dyslexia is a problem of primary school children that vanishes with the transition to second level. Only those children whose literacy attainments are at or below the 2nd percentile and whose ability is at the average level or above are entitled to resource teaching at second level.

Supports for students with dyslexia at second level are probably even more necessary than at primary level because of the wide range of subjects and teachers to which the student is exposed.

Completely new subjects, additional languages, a change of environment, frequent changes of classroom and timetables all create stress for the student with dyslexia. Not surprisingly, many students feel lost and unable to cope. A number will fail to make the transfer from primary to secondary schooling or will drop out prior to Junior Certificate. These are among the most vulnerable young people in society.

By mid-second level, state examinations loom for the student with dyslexia, bringing questions about which special accommodations to apply for and whether to avail of such arrangements, because these will be noted on the examination certificate.

So, though many reports have been published, legislation passed and circulars issued, all is not rosy in the garden of dyslexia. Some weeds, snags and traps for the unwary still remain. Many children with dyslexia are never identified and do not receive the specialist help they desperately need. Many drop out of school at an early age because they cannot cope with reading and writing. Early school leaving carries great risks for the future. Research in Britain and America reveals that a disproportionate number of prisoners are school dropouts with specific reading difficulties. At best, young people with no formal qualifications and poor literacy skills will be at the end of the queue when it comes to job opportunities. This is a preventable situation. Students with dyslexia can learn but they need to be taught appropriately and supported adequately.

The purpose of this book is to show how this can be achieved. It aims to highlight the importance of recognising dyslexia and dealing with it. The authors come from different disciplines and bring to the book their varied experience and training. Chapters 2, 3, 7 and 14 come from the pen of a psychologist, carrying the expertise and technical knowledge of the professional in this area. These chapters consider the definitions of dyslexia, the means of and issues around psychological assessment and report. Chapters 4, 8, 9, 10, 11 and 12, which deal with the formal educational aspects, are written by a serving second-level teacher. They provide a practical and informative approach to tackling day-to-day issues in the classroom. Chapters 1, 5, 6, 13, 15 and 16 are written by the Director of the Dyslexia Association of Ireland and derive from the knowledge and expertise accumulated from working for over twenty years with that organisation, lobbying, counselling and directing services for families, professionals and individuals. These chapters deal, in particular, with the child within the family and with dyslexia in adulthood. Two of the writers are parents of children with dyslexia.

The mix of practical knowledge, professional expertise and teaching experience will, it is hoped, offer information, understanding and advice to parents, teachers and adults about dyslexia, about the services that are available and how dyslexia can be set in context.

Naturally, some information may be more relevant to parents, some to teachers and some to students or adults with dyslexia. The authors have tried to indicate in chapter headings which section of the readership is being addressed but it is hoped that all the information is useful. Information has been checked for accuracy at the time of going to print but changes take place rapidly. Parents and teachers are advised to keep up-to-date with circulars issued by the Department of Education and Science and with developments in the field of dyslexia.

The positive message to people with dyslexia, their families and teachers is that dyslexia makes learning difficult but not impossible. Acquiring information about dyslexia, putting it in perspective and taking control of the learning situation can turn a potentially damaging disability into a manageable difficulty. It is hoped that this book will, for some, be the first step on the road to that achievement.

2. What Is Dyslexia?

This chapter will be of most use to parents, teachers and others who suspect that someone they know may have undiagnosed dyslexia or another specific learning difficulty. In it you will read about:

- Defining dyslexia;
- Main characteristics/indicators of dyslexia;
- Other specific learning difficulties.

Defining Dyslexia

Over the years since dyslexia was first recognised there have been numerous definitions and descriptions of what it is and how it can be identified. At first dyslexia was described as *word blindness*, then as *strephosymbolia* – meaning a *twisting of symbols* – and eventually as *dyslexia*. The word *dyslexia* comes from the Greek *dus/dys*, meaning *bad* or *difficult*, and *lexis*, meaning *word, vocabulary* or *language*. Thus *dyslexia* attests to a fundamental difficulty with language processing, particularly with written language.

For many years specific difficulty with the ability to read was studied as a medical condition. In 1877 it was identified by a German physician, Kussmaul, when writing of patients who had acquired a loss of ability to read. To describe it he used the term *word blindness*. Ten years later the word *dyslexia* was used for the same medical condition. It was not until the end of that century, circa 1896, that a general practitioner in Scotland, Pringle Morgan, wrote in the *British Medical Journal* of a fourteen-year-old boy who had great difficulty with reading and writing. The difference in the boy's case was that his difficulties did not occur as a result of some injury. Morgan concluded that his *word blindness* was congenital and was either inherited or acquired in the womb. By coincidence his article was published just several weeks after a Medical Officer in Yorkshire, James Kerr, noted in his report that some pupils who had no other learning difficulties appeared to have *congenital word blindness*, by which was meant difficulties specific to reading and writing which appear to be genetic.

A great deal more is now known about developmental dyslexia than was known at the time of Pringle Morgan. As research methods have developed, professionals in the field have come to understand that difficulty with reading and writing are external indicators of internal ways of processing information. Current research is directed at fundamental sensory and motor *processes*. Since reading and writing are relatively young skills on the human scale of evolution, being about 4,000 years old, it is theorised that these processes originally evolved for purposes other than reading and writing. This research into processes underlying reading and writing is an important direction to take. Identifying dyslexia as a clear biological condition means that children's delay and persisting difficulties in the reading and writing processes are recognised as real and part of who they are rather than the result of laziness, environmental or other external factors. Unfortunately, for many years – and occasionally today – dyslexia has been viewed as an *excuse*.

Dyslexia describes differences in the ways in which the individual processes written information. These differences make it more than usually difficult to learn to read, write and, sometimes, deal with numbers. On the other side, it is documented that people with dyslexia can be more advanced in the ways they see, understand and process *non-verbal* information and can be very creative and novel in problem solving. Dyslexia is an all-embracing term (some researchers refer to the *dyslexias*). It describes a complex of processing activities and abilities that come into play when one needs to read and write. These processes and abilities are also likely to affect how one learns, organises a task and deals with many everyday tasks. One *lives* with dyslexia. As it is not a medical problem it cannot be cured. As it is genetic it does not go away. The child and adult can adapt and find new ways to deal with information processing, thus getting around the original difficulties, often exploiting their strengths to do this.

Dyslexic difficulties can occur along a continuum from mild to severe. In any group of people with dyslexia there are a range of abilities and difficulties both within the individual and between the individuals. Some will have greater difficulty. Some will have greater ability. Usually the reading and writing delay is quite unexpected, given the individual's alertness and good ability in other aspects of learning.

Dyslexia can be described from a number of different perspectives: how one learns (*cognition*), what parts of the brain are involved (*neurology*), what genes are involved (*genetics*) and behaviour. What is known at the neurological and genetic levels is incomplete and the research is ongoing.

The definition of dyslexia adopted by the Board of Directors of the International Dyslexia Association is as follows:

> Dyslexia is a specific learning disability that is neurological in origin. It is characterized by difficulties with accurate and/or fluent word recognition and by poor spelling and decoding abilities. These difficulties typically result from a deficit in the phonological component of language that is often unexpected in relation to other cognitive abilities and the provision of effective classroom instruction. Secondary consequences may include problems in reading comprehension and reduced reading experience that can impede growth of vocabulary and background knowledge.
> (IDA, 2002)

Perhaps the definition that is most important to children is the one that recognises that dyslexia exists and that those who are dyslexic have special needs within the school system. The definitions used by education authorities are the bases for establishing rights under law and putting in place appropriate support systems in schools. They are descriptive and pragmatic rather than theoretic. When the Task Force on Dyslexia, set up by the Minister for Education and Science, published its report in July 2001, it defined dyslexia as follows:

> Dyslexia is manifested in a continuum of specific learning difficulties related to the acquisition of basic skills in reading, spelling and/or writing, such difficulties being unexpected in relation to an individual's other abilities and educational experiences. Dyslexia can be described at the neurological, cognitive and behavioural levels. It is typically characterised by inefficient information processing, including difficulties in phonological processing, working memory, rapid naming and automaticity of basic skills. Difficulties in organisation, sequencing and motor skills may also be present.

This describes dyslexia in terms of what is observed and what are recognised by researchers as the salient features of dyslexia. Dyslexia is manifested in the following ways:

- Unexpected difficulty with literacy and numbers;
- Difficulties in phonological awareness, i.e. ability to recognise the sound structures of a language;
- Poor auditory working memory;
- Delay in finding the right word (rapid naming);
- Delay in becoming automatic in a skill.

Children with dyslexia often experience other difficulties, such as poor co-ordination and fine motor movement, ability to sequence and organise, delay in learning time, mixed laterality and problems with accurate direction. A number of these indicators are common to many learning difficulties including dyslexia, dyspraxia, attention deficit hyperactivity disorders and specific language impairment.

The features described above may be seen as the main characteristics as far as they can be identified at this time. The Report of the Task Force acknowledged that it is not known exactly how visual processing is part of the picture. Children with dyslexia often experience difficulty with visual memory, eye tracking and reading speed. In the 1920s an American psychiatrist, Orton, noted that a significant number of children with reading difficulties reversed or inverted letters. His observations led to research on visual processing in children with dyslexia. Clearly, a reader must be able not only to know that language consists of combinations of sound and that words can be broken into sounds at different levels but also that these sounds are represented visually by a series of letters and let-ter-patterns. This recognition requires visual memory of words. Poor visual memory will result in writing letters in the wrong order and/or slower reading speed due to failure to recognise words automatically. The research studies of John Stein in Oxford have begun to identify differences in visual processing. Further studies on visual processing are taking place in Trinity College, Dublin at the time of going to press.

Main Characteristics/Indicators of Dyslexia

It was noted earlier that dyslexia does not go away. It is a way in which a person processes information. In the traditionally valued areas of linear thinking, order and sequencing and in the tasks of reading and writing the person with dyslexia can be significantly impaired. However, one must always remember that many individ-uals with dyslexia are very efficient/above average in how they process non-language information.

The ways in which dyslexia has an impact on day-to-day living tend to change over the years. In the early years difficulties with motor co-ordination, attention, learning phonics and the elementary tools for reading and writing predominate.

As the primary school child moves from junior to senior classes, issues around self-esteem and motivation may arise. Frustration and lack of self-confidence may interfere with social and emotional development. Difficulties with memory and organisation may com-pound delay in reading and writing.

In secondary school the challenge is to be able to deal with the range of subjects, the volume of reading and writing required and to prepare for and manage timed examinations. In addition they need to be able to look ahead to the future with confidence, know-ing that they have opportunities equal to those of their peers of fol-lowing the education and training courses that will best suit their talents and abilities. Literacy difficulties can dent their confidence, impair their level of performance and result in underachievement.

There are aspects of dyslexia which are constant and which do not go away when one leaves school: slower processing of audi-tory and visual information, difficulty with working memory, phono-logical difficulty, poor spelling and sometimes halting reading. Most adults with dyslexia have to use memos and calculators and a host of strategies to remind them of tasks to be done, names and numbers to be remembered and directions to be followed. Many continue to have difficulty attending to a long sermon or lecture or listening and writing simultaneously. Some will continue to be slow and halting when reading aloud. They can have difficulty in remembering people's names, addresses or telephone numbers. However, they will also have developed other learning skills and characteristics that stand them in good stead. Many adults with dyslexia are very thorough, because they leave nothing to chance. They plan carefully because they have to be prepared. Having had to spend a much longer time learning work at school, they have developed habits of diligence and know how to work much harder, if necessary, to accomplish a task. Often having struggled with their disability, they believe in their ability to achieve their goals.

While dyslexia is a difficulty, aspects of which are enduring, there are significant strengths associated with it. Those with dyslexia also often have particular strengths in visual perception and reasoning. Thomas G. West, author of *In the Mind's Eye*, proposes that the stronger visuo-spatial ability, which is evident in many people with dyslexia, is particularly suited to the modern world. The task for children, though, is to break through the barrier that delays their full access to knowledge in all its forms and to develop their innate abilities.

There are lists of indicators that may show that a dyslexic difficulty is present at the different stages in life. The first four lists are adapted from the Report of the Task Force on Dyslexia. The last list is taken from the Dyslexia Association of Ireland Information Booklet.

The lists are as follows:

- For children age three to five;
- For children age five to seven;
- For children age seven to twelve;
- For children age twelve plus;
- For adults.

Each child/adult with dyslexia has a unique profile of strengths and weaknesses. The lists of indicators help parents and teachers identify children who may have a dyslexic difficulty. An educational assessment will still be required to make a diagnosis. What the lists do is help to confirm the suspicions that there is a difficulty present and therefore help in making the decision to seek an assessment.

When looking at the lists of indicators, remember the following:

- No child will have all the indicators;
- Many children will have several of the indicators;

- Some indicators are more common than others;
- The number of indicators observed in a child does not indicate whether the child's dyslexia is mild, moderate or severe.

Indicators of possible learning difficulty arising from dyslexia (ages 3–5 years)
- Is later than most children in learning to speak;
- Has difficulty pronouncing some, especially multi-syllabic words;
- Has difficulty separating spoken words into sounds and blending spoken sounds to make words (i.e. has difficulty with phonological awareness);
- Experiences auditory discrimination problems;
- Is prone to spoonerisms (for example *'Fips and chish'* for *fish and chips*);
- Has difficulty with rhyming;
- Has difficulty maintaining rhythm;
- Is unable to recall the right word;
- Is slow to add new vocabulary;
- Exhibits delays in acquiring emergent literacy skills (for example understanding that written language progresses from left to right, discriminating between letters, words and sentences);
- Experiences problems learning the alphabet;
- Has trouble learning numbers, days of the week, colours and shapes;
- Has trouble learning to write and spell their name;
- Is unable to follow multi-step directions or routines;
- Is developing fine motor skills more slowly than other children;
- May have difficulty telling and/or retelling a story in correct sequence.

Indicators of a possible learning difficulty arising from dyslexia (ages 5–7 years)
- Is slow to learn the connection between letters and sounds (alphabetic principal);
- Has difficulty separating words into sounds and blending sounds to form words (phonemic awareness);
- Has difficulty repeating multi-syllabic words (for example *'emeny'* for *enemy*, *'pasghetti'* for *spaghetti*);
- Has difficulty decoding single words (reading single words in isolation);
- Has poor word-attack skills, especially for new words;
- Confuses small or easy words: *at/to; said/and; does/goes*;
- May make constant reading and spelling errors including:
    - Letter reversals (for example *d* for *b* as in *dog* for *bog*)
    - Letter inversions (for example *m* for *w*)

- Letter transpositions (for example *felt* and *left*)
- Word reversals (for example *tip* for *pit*)
- Word substitutions (for example *house* for *home*);
- Reads slowly with little expression or fluency (oral reading is slow and laborious);
- Has more difficulty with function words (for example *is, to, of*) than with content words (for example *clouds, run, yellow*);
- May be slow to learn new skills, relying heavily on memorising without understanding;
- Reading comprehension is below expectation due to poor accuracy, fluency and speed;
- Reading comprehension is better than single-word reading;
- Listening comprehension is better than reading comprehension;
- Has trouble learning facts;
- Has difficulty planning or organising;
- Uses awkward pencil grip;
- Has slow and poor quality handwriting;
- Has trouble learning to tell the time on an analogue clock or watch;
- Has poor fine motor co-ordination.

Indicators of a possible learning difficulty arising from dyslexia (ages 7–12 years)
- Has continued difficulty reading text aloud or silently;
- Reading achievement is below expectation;
- Still confuses letter sequences (for example *'soiled'* for *solid*; *'left'* for *felt*);
- Is slow at discerning and learning prefixes, suffixes, root words and other morphemes as part of reading and spelling strategies;
- Poor reading accuracy, fluency or speed interferes with reading comprehension;
- Spelling is inappropriate for age and general ability (for example spelling the same word differently on the same page, use of bizarre spelling patterns, frequent letter omissions, additions and transposition);
- Poor spelling contributes to poor written expression (for example may avoid use of unfamiliar words);
- Use avoidance tactics when asked to read orally or write;
- Experiences language-related problems in Maths (for example when reading word problems and directions, confuses numbers and symbols);
- Is unable to learn multiplication tables by rote;
- Still confuses some directional words (for example left and right);
- Has slow or poor recall of facts;

- Lacks understanding of other people's body language and facial expressions;
- Has trouble with non-literal or figurative language (for example idioms, proverbs);
- Forgets to bring in or hand in homework;
- Has difficulty remembering what day or month it is;
- Has difficulty remembering their telephone number or birthday;
- Has poor planning and organisational skills;
- Has poor time management;
- Lacks self-confidence and has a poor self-image.

Indicators of a possible learning difficulty arising from dyslexia (ages 12 years+)
- Is still reading slowly and without fluency, with many inaccuracies;
- Misreads words (for example *hysterical* for *historical*) or information;
- Has difficulty modifying reading rate;
- Has an inadequate store of knowledge due to lack of reading experience;
- Continues to experience serious spelling difficulties;
- Has slow, dysfluent and/or illegible handwriting;
- Has better oral skills than written skills;
- Has difficulty planning, sequencing and organising written text;
- Has difficulty with written syntax or punctuation;
- Has difficulty skimming, scanning and/or proofreading written text;
- Has trouble summarising or outlining;
- Has problems in taking notes and copying from the board;
- Procrastinates and/or avoids reading and writing tasks;
- Does not complete assignments or class work or does not hand them in;
- Is slow in answering questions, especially open-ended ones;
- Has poor memorisation skills;
- Still mispronounces or misuses some words;
- Has problems recalling the names of some words or objects;
- Has poor planning and organisation skills;
- Has poor time-management skills;
- Has more difficulty with language-based subjects (for example English, Irish, History) than with non-language-based subjects (for example Mathematics, Technical Graphics);
- Lacks self-confidence and has poor self-image.

Indicators of a possible learning difficulty arising from dyslexia in adults

- Difficulty with reading aloud;
- Difficulty with reading unfamiliar material;
- Tendency to mispronounce or misread words;
- Slow pace of reading;
- Reading for information only, not for pleasure;
- Understanding more easily when listening than when reading;
- Difficulty with spelling;
- Finding it hard to visualise words or remember the sequence of letters in a word;
- Difficulty with sentence construction and punctuation;
- Difficulty putting information on paper;
- Difficulty in spotting mistakes made in written work;
- Finding it easier to express thoughts in words than in writing;
- Underachieving at school, particularly in exams;
- Having immature or ill-formed handwriting;
- Tendency to be clumsy and uncoordinated;
- Confusing left and right;
- Finding it hard to remember things in sequence;
- Difficulty in remembering new information or new names;
- Getting phone messages wrong;
- Confusion with times, dates and appointments;
- Getting phone numbers wrong by perhaps reversing digits;
- Making 'silly' mistakes in calculations;
- Having 'good' days and 'bad' days;
- Poor short-term memory;
- Having close family members with dyslexia.

EDUCATIONAL RESOURCES

Other Specific Learning Difficulties

The term *dyslexia* is often written as being synonymous with the terms *specific learning difficulties/specific learning disability*. This can be very confusing. The term *specific learning disability* includes dyslexia as one of a number of *specific*, as distinct from *general*, learning disabilities. Dyslexia is specific to certain aspects of learning. Very often the person with reading difficulty scores on an intelligence scale in the average or above-average ranges. The difficulties are not the result of overall general learning disability. Psychologists in reports often describe a child as *having a specific learning difficulty of a dyslexic nature.*

The term *specific learning disability* has a wider meaning than dyslexia. It is used to encompass a number of specific disabilities that co-exist with average to high functioning in other cognitive areas. Since the mid-1990s the term has been used to include dyslexia, dyspraxia, specific language impairment (SLI), attention deficit disorder (ADD)/attention deficit hyperactivity disorder (ADHD) and autistic spectrum disorder. When observing and, later, assessing for each of these syndromes, one is aware of the overlap of many of the features of dyslexia. Thus the child with dyspraxia has difficulty similar to that of the child with dyslexia in processing information, with memory, laterality, following instructions, attention, sense of direction, sequencing, copying from the board and concept of time. However, the core deficit of dyslexia, co-existing with some or all of the above, is difficulty with decoding the written word and with spelling. The core deficit in the child with dyspraxia is difficulty with motor co-ordination. The core deficit for ADD/ADHD is with attention and impulse control. The core deficit with specific language impairment is with language comprehension and creating sentences.

As a response to this awareness that a great number of difficulties are common to several co-occurring disabilities, researchers are considering the possibility that there may in fact be one underlying impairment rather than separate 'conditions'. Kaplan et al (1998) suggest the term *atypical brain development*. They see the need to assess pupils and students across a wide spectrum of tests because of the difficulties of not having discrete indicators for each disability. A wide and full assessment is necessary to make sure the child is appropriately diagnosed. This may sometimes require the child to be seen by the educational psychologist and one or more of the following: the speech and language therapist, the occupational therapist or the psychiatrist. Studies indicate that the co-occurrence of one or more disabilities is relatively high. Portwood (1999) has suggested that between 40 and 45 per cent of children with dyspraxia have co-occurring dyslexia. Hynd (2002) suggests that around 50 per cent of children with dyslexia also have ADHD. Snowling's work on reading has indicated the overlap between language impairment and dyslexia. Her research showed that children with reading impairment at age eight showed a pattern of oral speech and language delay in pre-school years.

Of these disabilities dyslexia is probably the most recognised. However, because many parents may be unsure of how these co-existing conditions are observable, the following brief explanations are included here. More detailed information about these specific learning difficulties and with regard to assessment and support can best be obtained from the relevant organisations. Details of contact addresses can be found at the end of this chapter.

Dyspraxia

The term *dyspraxia* comes from the root *dus/dys* meaning *bad* or *difficult* and *praxis* meaning *movement* or *action*. Developmental dyspraxia is the term used to describe a condition whereby the child has more than usual difficulty with co-ordination, with organising movement and also often has significant visual perceptual difficulties. In some literature it can be referred to as *developmental co-ordination disorder* (DCD). The difficulties the child experiences are not caused by other recognised conditions, such as cerebral palsy, multiple sclerosis or hemiplegia. In early childhood the features most noticeable include:

- Difficulty articulating words;
- Difficulty dressing oneself;
- Limited concentration;
- Difficulty following instructions;
- Sensitivity to noise and changing light;
- Difficulty with spatial perception resulting in bumping into things, being clumsy and falling over easily.

Attention Deficit/Hyperactivity Disorders (ADD and ADHD)

ADD/ADHD describes a condition where the child has more than usual difficulty maintaining attention for any length of time, is highly distractible, disorganised, forgetful and appears not to listen to instructions. These children may also be over-active, fidgety, want everything instantly and be impulsive. Many people associate ADHD with hyperactivity, i.e. they focus on the most obvious indicator, the child's difficulty staying still and the need to be constantly 'on the go'. However, since 1994, a significant distinction has been made between ADD and ADHD. In the first case the child does not exhibit the *hyper* activity of the second case. In both cases the core difficulty is with ability to control attention.

The following is a checklist of some of the items that describe a child with ADD:

- Difficulty concentrating, except on activities of personal interest;
- Highly distractible;
- Inconsistent – good days/bad days;
- Disorganised;
- Difficulty following through instructions;
- Poor perseverance except on tasks enjoyed;
- Pays little attention to detail;
- Forgetful and dreamy.

In addition to the above, the child with ADHD manifests behaviours such as the following:

- Unable to stay seated for any length of time;
- Fidgety, restless and constantly touching things;
- Asks questions impulsively, interrupts, makes inappropriate comments and/or makes vocal noises;
- Needs to be moving most of the time;
- Has difficulty in controlling impulses;
- Can be impatient and demanding of instant response;
- Cannot queue in lines;
- Acts first, thinks later.

As with dyslexia and dyspraxia, any two children with ADHD/ADD may have quite different profiles because their combination of difficulties places them at different points along a continuum of difficulties. It is important to note that their poor reading and writing development may not be rooted in dyslexia but may result from their difficulty focusing attention long enough to get a grasp of basic instructions.

Asperger's Syndrome

The term *Asperger's Syndrome* came into use as recently as 1983, in a paper published by Burgoine and Wing that describes the features that are considered to characterise the disability. In the 1940s a Viennese paediatrician, Hans Asperger, had already identified these, hence the name. Asperger's Syndrome is usually classified under the Autistic Spectrum Disorders. In the United States and in some English-speaking countries it is referred to as 'high-functioning autism'. Asperger's Syndrome/Disorder describes the social components of autism but without the significant impairments of learning and language that characterise autism.

The following are the core features of Asperger's Syndrome:

- Lack of empathy;
- Poor ability to form friendships;
- One-sided conversations;
- Intense absorption in a special interest;
- Poor verbal communication;
- Odd postures and clumsy movements.

It should be remembered that the presence of any one or any cluster of these features does not in itself indicate Asperger's Disorder: for example, poor communication skills and consequently poor ability to hold a two-sided conversation may be caused by a language disorder. The only way to get a true diagnosis is to have an appropriate assessment that is wide-ranging and thorough. *Aspire*, the Asperger's Syndrome organisation, will provide advice on where to look for this.

Specific Language Impairment (SLI)

Although specific language impairment (SLI) is not strictly classified as a specific learning difficulty, many children with dyslexia have experienced specific language delay. They may have required speech therapy, usually at the pre-school and kindergarten stage. Specific language delay can occur in either or both of the areas of expression and reception. The difficulties may be at the level of phonology (discrimination of different sounds, recognition of similar sounds), semantics (understanding meaning), syntax (grammatical structure of sentence), pragmatics (using language suited to what they want to communicate) and fluency. Recent studies in Britain by Professor Margaret Snowling have identified reading comprehension difficulties in significant numbers of children. The studies also suggest that children with poor oral language skills are at high risk of literacy failure. Dyslexia and language difficulties often co-exist. This is why a psychologist assessing for dyslexia may sometimes recommend a further assessment by a speech and language therapist.

In the following chapter you will receive more detailed information with regard to assessment.

Contact Addresses

The Dyspraxia Association, 69A Main Street, Leixlip, Co. Kildare,
  Tel: 01 2957125, Website: www.dyspraxiaireland.com.
HADD (for Attention Deficit Disorders), Carmichael House,
  North Brunswick Street, Dublin 7, Tel: 01 8748349 (Wednes-
  day/Friday mornings).
Aspire (for Autistic Spectrum Disorders), Carmichael House,
  North Brunswick Street, Dublin 7, Tel: 01 8780027, Website:
  www.aspire-irl.com.

3. Screening and Assessment

This chapter will be of most use to parents and teachers and is about formally identifying dyslexia. What should happen when you begin to feel concerned that the child is having more than usual difficulty with sounds, letters and words? In this chapter you will read about the following:

- Identifying dyslexia through a staged approach;
- The psycho-educational assessment;
- Understanding the assessment report;
- Questions following assessment;
- Review of progress and reassessment;
- Standardised testing in schools.

Identifying Dyslexia through a Staged Approach

In educational circles the current most popularly accepted process for identification of dyslexia is a co-operative, staged approach. Such an approach is set out in the Department of Education and Science Learning Support Guidelines (2000), where parents and professionals are in close communication to ensure early identification and appropriate intervention. The assessment begins with the class teacher. The class teacher consults the specialist teacher, namely the special needs teacher. The special needs teacher refers the child on to the psychologist and other specialists, if necessary. The parents need to be involved from the beginning and should be consulted at each stage of the process. For example, the parent may become aware of difficulties through the nightly struggle with homework. By sharing this knowledge with the classroom teacher greater vigilance can be maintained.

Not all reading delay is caused by dyslexia and, as children develop at different rates, one is reluctant to diagnose dyslexia before the child is seven years old. However, once the parent or the teacher begins to feel there is a possible reading delay, it is wise to talk about it and put interventions in place. Some children are more at risk, for example those who have other members of their family with dyslexia.

Stage One in identifying pupils who are experiencing difficulty and delay is for the classroom teacher to administer one or more screening tests to identify the particular nature of the difficulty in relation to the learning that is expected to have taken place at this stage of the child's development. Based on the information gained from this an individual pupil learning programme (IPLP) is drawn up. Learning Support Guidelines contain detailed information about such programmes and recommend that the school involves the parent in 'contributing to the development and implementation of their child's IPLP'. An IPLP is a record of relevant information. It notes present levels of attainment and identifies learning strengths and needs. It forms the basis for setting goals to be reached and the means to achieve them. It should be revised at each stage.

Stage Two involves putting learning support in place. This means that the child is withdrawn from the general classroom for a short period of the day and given additional tuition. Progress is monitored and the level of progress is assessed by objective tests at the end of a period of specific instruction, usually thirteen or twenty weeks. The IPLP is revised according to the progress registered.

Stage Three is when the parent and the teacher are relatively sure that there is more than maturational delay responsible for the child's struggle with sounds, letters and words. The school requests written permission to have the child referred for psycho-educational assessment by the psychologist assigned to the school under the National Educational Psychological Service (NEPS). The psychologist carries out the assessment in the school.

The staged approach is designed to ensure that the child's progress is carefully monitored and appropriate remedial tuition is put in place. Ideally it should lead to children with dyslexia receiving a better service.

Of course, it is also possible to have a child assessed by a psychologist who works privately or as part of the service offered by the Dyslexia Association of Ireland. In these cases appointments can be made directly with the psychologist and it is not necessary to wait for Stage Three. The assessment takes place usually in the psychologist's place of work or in the DAI offices in Suffolk Street. A list of practising psychologists may be obtained from the Psychological Society of Ireland (www.psihq.ie).

The Psycho-Educational Assessment

Assessment serves more purposes than naming the cause of a child's difficulties. It is closely related to intervention. On the one hand it is intended to be a way of pin-pointing where the areas of specific difficulty lie and what aspects of literacy learning need to be targeted for additional tuition. It also aims to explore how the child learns and to identify strengths in how learning and information processing take place. Children suspected of having dyslexia often display an incongruous mix of abilities and disabilities.

Dyslexia is not all negative and the assessment is about more than identifying deficits. These children may have considerable strengths and may be very creative and adept at non-verbal pursuits, finding ways around problems and using strategies. However, the difficulties may significantly affect how a child learns. Identifying learning strengths and weaknesses is the key to opening up different ways of learning. The psycho-educational assessment is essentially an exploration of cognitive functioning, looking at how faculties such as memory, assimilation, reasoning and language are developing. It tries to measure the child's abilities and compare how that child is functioning with what is the norm for that child's age group.

More importantly, perhaps, it indicates how particular abilities, known to be weak on the profiles of children with dyslexia, compare with the child's other abilities. Over the years test materials have been developed scientifically to try to do this. What makes the psycho-educational assessment different from the tests of reading, writing, spelling and mathematics in school is the scope of the assessment. It measures not simply the level of attainment but tries to identify functions of processing that make sense of patterns of reading and spelling behaviour.

A full psycho-educational assessment aims to gather as much background information as possible about the child. It is important to understand the child in relation to the family and progress at school. Thus a very important aspect of the assessment is the interview between the psychologist and the parents – both parents, if possible. Questions may be asked about family history and the child's early development, health, eyesight and hearing. Before diagnosing dyslexia, it is important to rule out any possibility that poor vision or hearing deficits are the primary cause of the child's difficulty: for example, children who have had grommets inserted may be slower to pick up the subtle differences of letter-sounds.

It is also important for the psychologist to get as full a report as possible from the child's class and learning support teachers in order to be informed about how the child works in a familiar setting and on a daily basis. Remember, the psychologist is meeting the child for the first time, for a limited amount of time and, sometimes, out of a familiar environment.

As a parent, you may ask to be present throughout the assessment. If parents wish to stay, they will be placed to the back of the room, out of their child's field of vision, and excluded from taking any active part or intervening in any way, unless the child is anxious. However, it is usually better for parents to leave, so that distraction caused by their presence is reduced. The psychologist guides the child through a series of tasks, some oral, some written, some practical and some visual with the intention of getting knowledge about overall ability, working memory, verbal and visuo-spatial ability. Tests to assess the level of word reading, reading comprehension, spelling and mathematics are also given and, if time permits, some exploration of ability to express ideas, both orally and in written form.

The assessment includes checking the child's facility with the tools and structure of language and with phonological awareness. This means checking if the child can do the following:

- Understand that words are composed of sounds blended together;
- Identify similar/dissimilar sounds;
- Match sounds with corresponding letters or letter patterns.

The psychologist may look for other information if there are suspicions that features of co-existing conditions are present, such as dyspraxia, specific language disorder or attention deficit disorder. If this is the case, additional tests will be administered to check out attention levels or fine motor movement, visual difficulties and laterality. A full psycho-educational assessment may take one or two sessions to complete.

Following assessment there is often an opportunity for some immediate feedback. If the assessment is done in school this may not be possible for the parent so, in this case, feedback is given to the teacher or school principal and an alternative date can be given for feedback to the parent. Often a psychologist prefers to work through the test results before making definitive diagnoses and recommendations.

The psychologist arrives at a conclusion deduced from all the information gleaned from the interview, test results, observed behaviours and school reports. It is important to remember that while the psychologist tries to have as near ideal conditions as possible, these tests are also subject to human error. Ultimately the results reflect how the child was on the day, under the particular circumstances.

Understanding the Assessment Report

A report is then written up and sent to the parent; if the assessment was done in school the report is sent to the school principal and the parent gets a copy. The report contains a variety of information. Some of the language may be technical and specialised and so one should not hesitate to ask for explanations. The report is written with two readers in mind: the parent and the teacher. The parent wants to know what conclusion the psychologist has reached and what interventions should now ensue. The teacher may expect to find sufficiently detailed information, recommendations and guidelines for writing up the child's individual profile and learning programme.

There is no standard way of writing a report and each psychologist will have a personal writing style and ease of communication. Some reports are more formal and technical than others. This is because the psychologist intends to give as much information as possible to the different readers of the report. You should always feel you can ask the psychologist to talk you through the report.

Besides the parent and teacher, this report may need to be seen by other specialists if, for example, the child needs to be referred for further assessment to a paediatrician, a speech therapist or an occupational therapist. The report will be required by the Department of Education and Science if the decision is taken to apply for an exemption from Irish and/or reasonable accommodation in exams. It is also needed by the Disability Support Officers at third-level if application is made to access these services. There is considerable discussion at the time of going to press around the question of standardising reports, especially those needed when a student is transferring from second- to third-level education.

The following is one example of what a psycho-educational report may include:

Background

The report incorporates those pieces of information that relate to the reasons why an assessment was requested, what background information is relevant and salient information from teachers' reports. The psychologist wants to know if other members of the family have similar difficulties and how the child behaves in the home. Also included is the child's own perception of school learning and difficulties.

Developmental history, medical conditions or history of sensory deficits and language development are noted. Reports from teachers with regard to difficulties, results of tests administered and reports of progress, what intervention programmes are in place and whether or not the child is receiving additional tuition in or outside school forms part of this background. It is also useful to include an account of perceived strengths.

As this report, while being confidential, will be read by persons outside the family there may be some information you share with the psychologist that you do not wish to be written into the report. It is important to indicate this at the time.

Observations

This section includes observations made by the psychologist about the child with regard to such features as ease of separation from the parent, interaction with the psychologist, learning style, ability to persevere at a task, writing, taking in spoken instructions, learning strategies being used and ability to sustain attention over time. Each of these gives valuable information to support test results and ultimately helps the psychologist to arrive at a final conclusion.

Tests administered

This section contains a list of the various tests administered. Again there is no standard battery of tests but all educational assessments include tests of general intellectual ability and literacy attainments. Often, but not always, a written mathematics test is also included. Some test materials have greater reliability than others. This is because they have been tested on large numbers of children of all ages and backgrounds before being released for general use. One can have a high degree of confidence that they give an accurate indication of the child's current functioning.

Test results

This section describes the results of the tests administered. The intelligence tests generally used are the Wechsler Intelligence Scale and the British Ability Scales. Each of these tests consists of a number of verbal, non-verbal and visuo-spatial tests. Visuo-spatial tests require no language from the child. They test ability to take in, remember and analyse visual and spatial information. When the individual scores on each of the scales are calculated together, they give an indication of overall level of ability or IQ score. Older IQ tests also give a verbal IQ and a non-verbal IQ. The most recent edition of the WISC provides four index scores: verbal comprehension, perceptual reasoning, working memory and processing speed.

A note about IQ tests and scores, as many people can find these very confusing and misleading: IQ tests are constructed in such a way that each test consists of a number of items that are ranged in order from easy to difficult. Thus the same test can be used for all ages – the older the children, the more items they are expected to complete. When IQ tests are being constructed they are piloted on very large numbers of children. As a result, it is possible to ascertain a level of functioning that is *average* for each age group. It then becomes possible to describe a child's level of intelligence as being in the *average*, *high average* or *low average* range. These categories relate to what might be expected in a general population. Table 3.1 shows the range of IQ scores which reflects the Normal Distribution Curve. This curve is a statistical concept based on the fact that if a normal population of people, chosen at random, were tested, their IQ scores would fall across a range of scores according to a very specific pattern. This pattern, or distribution, applies to any normal population. On a graph the results form an even curve, which is generally referred to as the Normal Distribution Curve. In terms of scores, an IQ score of 100 is considered to be the mid-point. Fifty per cent of the population will have IQ scores between 90 and 109. This is the *average* range. A similar curve is applicable to standard scores where the mid-point, again, is 100. IQ scores are calculated according to what might be expected of a child, depending on that child's age. Thus, each test is constructed in such a way that there are a number of items on each test that one would expect a child of that age to be able to complete. If children complete a number of items beyond what is expected of an *average* child of their age, then their ability is described as being in the *high average, high* or *exceptionally high* range. If they complete fewer items they are described as being in the *low average, low* or *exceptionally low* range.

These categories such as *average* or *low average* refer to a range of scores within which the child may be said to be functioning at the time of testing. The term *range* rather than a *number* is a better way of describing the child's level of ability. This allows for a margin of error on the day, given that both the psychologist and the child are fallible beings!

The ranges correspond to the scores known as IQ scores. The middle point of the average range is an IQ of 100. Scores divide in the following way:

Table 3.1: IQ scores

IQ score	IQ range
130 and above	Exceptionally high
120–129	High
110–119	High average
90–109	Average
80–89	Low average
70–79	Low
Below 70	Exceptionally low

Scores can also be written as *percentiles.* Percentiles describe where, in a typical group of 100 children of the same age, the child would be placed in terms of achievement on a particular task, group of tasks and ability. Thus the child placed at the 90th percentile will achieve as well or better than 90 children out of the 100. Similarly, if the child is at the 45th percentile, achievement will be as good as or better than 45 in the group of 100.

Sometimes a report quotes *scaled scores.* These refer to the individual subtest results. An example is the child's performance on the individual subtests of the Wechsler Intelligence Scale for Children (WISC), which is scored on a scale of 1–19. Average is in the range 8–12. Any scaled score above 12 is *above average.* Any score below 8 is *below average.* As scores approach the score of 19, this is an indication of increasing strength of ability. Similarly as scores approach 1, they are indicators of increasing difficulty. The scaled scores are added up and converted to obtain the IQ scores. Scaled scores are calculated for each age group. If a child aged eight years and five months gets ten items correct, a scaled score of fifteen is attained, but if a child of twelve years and three months gets those same ten items complete, the scaled score is closer to nine.

From this section of the report you should get a good idea of where the child's strengths lie and also where there may be a need to develop abilities. You should also get an idea of whether verbal ability is stronger than non-verbal ability or vice versa. This is pertinent information. Teaching methods will be most successful when a child's strengths are used to best effect and when weaknesses are recognised and remediation put in place. It is through the strengths that a child will be able to make good progress, maintain self-confidence and learn ways around the difficulty.

There are a number of subtests that are more difficult than others for children with dyslexia. On the WISC subtests they often score lower on *Information, Arithmetic, Coding, Digit Span* and *Symbol Search,* compared with the subtests *Vocabulary, Similarities* and *Block Design.* The tasks in the first five of these subtests need particular abilities which research has shown are weaker in persons with dyslexia. These abilities include:

- Auditory working memory;
- Visual short-term memory;
- Visual discrimination, i.e. being able very quickly to see differences in visual symbols. This skill is very important for reading;
- Speed of processing.

As research uncovers more information about the differences in dyslexic processing, test instruments are becoming more refined and better able to identify these areas. WISC 4, for example, has introduced new tests that are better measures of working memory and processing speed. The emphasis is on functioning rather than score achieved.

Attainments

The term *Attainments* refers to the levels of reading, spelling and numeracy that the child has attained. This section of the report contains analysis of tests of word recognition, spelling, reading comprehension and word attack skills. It is possible for the psychologist to check from statistics the reading and mathematical scores that are appropriate for each ability and age level.

As with the IQ tests, literacy and numeracy test scores have been *standardised*. This means they have been tried out on large numbers of children across all sections of a society. In this way it becomes possible to say what the average child of any given age should be able to read, spell and calculate. The results of these literacy and numeracy tests are quoted in *standard scores*. These are similar to IQ scores in that a standard score of 100 is the mid-point of the *Average* range.

Attainment test results are also often quoted in age equivalents. This means instead of giving a standard score, the report records a *reading age*. While reading ages are useful, they can also be very misleading. Usually reading ability corresponds to level of intellectual functioning. Thus, a child of age six with an average IQ would be expected to have a reading age of six years. But if the child's ability is above or below average, the reading age may not be the same as the chronological age. A six year-old child with an IQ of 115 would be expected to have a reading age of seven years.

It is possible to predict from an IQ score what standard score you might expect a child at any particular age to have obtained. If there is a significant gap/discrepancy between the predicted score and the score attained on the day's testing, which cannot be explained by any other cause such as a long absence from school on account of illness, then a diagnosis of dyslexia is most likely.

Significant means that the discrepancy is *unusually* wide. Some discrepancy is allowed for but there are cut-off points beyond which the psychologist concludes that this discrepancy needs to be explained by more than the usual variations found among children of this age.

This ability/attainment discrepancy has long been an important feature in the diagnosis of dyslexia. It is not without controversy but it is used widely by most education authorities in Ireland, the United States and Britain to help diagnose dyslexia.

While scores and reading ages are necessary, it should also be remembered that at every assessment the psychologist is looking at how the child is functioning. This is a much more important question than what score does the child achieve. Scores in themselves are very inadequate descriptions of a child's learning ability and potential. The purpose of the assessment is to make recommendations to improve the child's way of learning. Thus attainment scores should be read in conjunction with a description of *how* the child is reading or writing.

The types of reading tests given may vary according to the age of the child. With older children the psychologist needs to assess their reading rate as well as accuracy. It is necessary to check out how automatically children can sound out a letter, a syllable and a polysyllabic word. These are called word-attack skills and testing is usually done by asking children to read nonsense words that are made of patterns similar to real words. This ensures that children are not reading from the memory of a word but can actually relate sound with symbol and patterns of symbols. The reading test checks children's ease of word recognition and a reading comprehension exercise checks how efficiently they can read sentences and if they are using context to read.

The assessment also tests the child's spelling knowledge. The advantage of standardised tests which are not in general use in school is that they test the child's long-term memory of spelling of words which are in familiar usage but not directly related to the day's or week's classroom activities. Passages of free writing and dictation may also be given to see if knowledge of spelling transfers to these activities. Writing speed is an important piece of information about the older children and is essential when looking at their need for supports in examinations or at third level.

Tests of level of numeracy may or may not be included in every assessment. The general ability subtests include an oral arithmetic test, which gives some indication of the child's understanding of number and numerical operations. Of course, if Maths is an area of difficulty in school or when doing homework, this should be reported to the psychologist in the initial interview.

Phonological awareness, sequencing, laterality, directionality

Further sections in the report may discuss other abilities such as phonological awareness, sequencing, laterality and directionality. Investigating these throws much light on aspects of the child's abilities. These are often areas of difficulty that can be indicative of dyslexia, though not peculiar to dyslexia only.

Phonological awareness is the ability to break down words into separate sounds, to play with sounds, to recognise similar sounds in words, to exchange sounds, to add and subtract sounds from words such as *slight/sight* and to hear the difference. Difficulties in the area of phonological awareness are now recognised as one of the core features of dyslexia.

Tests of memory such as reciting the order of the days of the week, months of the year, arithmetical tables and the alphabet are recorded as sequencing ability.

Laterality refers to which hand, foot or eye a child uses in preference to the other. Sometimes the child may not yet have established dominance. With others there may be cross-laterality, for example they may use right hand and foot but left eye. Recognising this may be important for the direction their eye follows when presented with tasks such as reading.

Directionality is noted in the report when the psychologist refers to the child's ability to identify directions right/left.

Summary and recommendations

The final section of the report states the conclusion at which the psychologist has arrived and the recommendations made in the light of the child's needs. These recommendations should be incorporated into the school's plan for the child.

However, the report is not only for the school. There are many ways a child's abilities can be developed at home in a less formal way through games and family activities (see Chapter 7). The report and the recommendations should be read carefully and a home plan of action drawn up which complements what will happen at school. This is where working very closely with the school is the best approach. As a parent, you are not expected to take on the role of teacher and the school cannot substitute for the emotional and practical support only a parent can give to the child. Parents and teachers can help one another by sharing information, reinforcing lessons, creating structures, negotiating volume of work and making sure that all the other aspects of the child's life are being developed.

Apart from recommendations for remediation at school and implementation at home, the psychologist may recommend that you consult specialists in other areas in order to investigate further some issues raised by the assessment. Dyslexia is only one of a number of learning difficulties. There tend to be a number of these difficulties that co-exist. Some dyslexic children may have aspects of dyspraxia, attention deficit disorder or Asperger's syndrome. In this case it will be necessary to make an appointment with the relevant specialists. The psycho-educational assessment may well be only the first of a number of assessment procedures. The diagnosis of attention deficit disorder is usually made in a medical context. Dyspraxia is identified through occupational therapy. Many children require speech and language assessments.

Questions Following the Assessment

After the assessment the following are some questions that may arise for parents.

How am I likely to respond when my suspicions that my child has a learning difficulty are confirmed by the psychologist?

For most people knowing is more comfortable than not knowing, even if it means one is in for the 'long haul' and that there are no 'quick fixes'. The essential facts about you and your child have not changed. You have always lived with a child who learns in a definite way. What is going to change is the way that learning style must be accommodated in the family and in the classroom. You and the family members will probably need to learn more about dyslexia. As already suggested, you will have to work even more closely with teachers. You may have to find out what additional supports may be available in and outside school. You may have worries about how other people will accept and deal with the idea that your child has dyslexia. Knowledge and information are the best tools for countering fears. Fortunately discussion about dyslexia is much more in the public domain now, so one can expect greater acceptance and understanding in society. The video/CD ROM/DVD *Understanding Dyslexia* produced by the Department of Education and Science in 2005 should further heighten awareness and understanding (available from Government Publications).

How am I going to explain to my child what dyslexia is?

Your child already knows that learning is a struggle when many in the class group are speeding ahead. How much you can tell children depends to a degree on their level of understanding and psychological readiness. In general it is better for you to explain in a positive way before somebody else does, perhaps in not so supportive an environment. Dyslexia is about different ways of learning. Your child has strengths, not only those that were assessed but many others that were not included in assessment. What is essential is that you remain positive about your child's ability, potential and the long-term outcomes, about your ability to provide guidance and that you encourage your child to grow in confidence.

How do I explain to the child's brothers and sisters?

As with the child, the more siblings are encouraged to respect difference, the more they understand. Dyslexia should be presented not so much emphasising the difficulties but allowing the child with dyslexia to demonstrate abilities. It is necessary to reinforce the knowledge that we each have *disabilities*, just as we have abilities. They may need to understand that the ability to learn to read and write at an early age is not the only, or the most important, aspect of being a capable person.

The psycho-educational assessment is the most accurate way we have at this time of identifying learning difficulties. It is not infallible. Remember, no test instrument is perfect. The psychologist will encourage children to do the best they can and to be at ease. However, both child and psychologist can be influenced by such factors as tiredness, anxiety or even environmental factors such as the noise level, time of day or the comfort of surroundings. In the assessment procedure one tries as much as possible to keep these external variables to a minimum. The language used to introduce the various subtests is laid down by the test constructors so that the instructions given to a child do not vary from psychologist to psychologist. There are time rules for many of the items. When these have been observed to the best ability of child and psychologist, the assessment is deemed to be valid. In the end, the judgements made and conclusions arrived at are, at best, good estimations based on reliable test materials, the psychologist's knowledge and experience, and how the child presented on the day.

Review of Progress and Reassessment

Review of progress

In primary school, once your child has had dyslexia identified through assessment, it should happen as a matter of course that an IPLP will be set up. Review of progress will be part of this programme. The difficulty may be that in some cases where a child does not receive additional support, this may not be provided and the main testing in school may be through the standard end-of-year tests. In reality the child would benefit from a more detailed assessment of gains and losses over the year and this needs a more diagnostic review.

At second level the student's needs are different from those in primary school. However, it is necessary to continue to identify these as the child goes through the school system. The student's progress should be discussed regularly with their teachers. If a review cannot be facilitated in school a specialist tutor or the psychologist who made the diagnosis could be asked to review progress.

Reassessment

Some people like to have their children reassessed regularly. In general, a full reassessment should be necessary only at critical points in the child's academic career. It may be advisable before transferring from primary to secondary school, particularly if the first assessment was carried out when the child was in first or second class. Profiles tend to change as the child becomes older.

A recent assessment (one less than two years old) is usually required when applying for reasonable accommodations in the Leaving Certificate or for accessing disability services at third level. Other than on these occasions a full assessment should only be considered in the light of individual cases.

Standardised Testing in Schools

In July 2005 the Minister for Education, Ms Mary Hanafin, announced plans for the introduction of standardised testing for all seven- and eleven-year-old pupils in primary schools. Parents will receive a report card detailing how their child has performed in relation to national averages. The plan is to introduce the new system in the 2007–2008 academic year.

However, it is important to realise that there are very real limitations to the use of standardised testing for students with dyslexia.

Standardised tests are tests given under very strict conditions. The purpose of each test is to give a result that shows how a student achieved in relation to the population of students of the same age. This is done by comparing the result to norms that have been researched. Standardised tests in use in Irish schools include the Micra T tests, Drumcondra Tests, Differential Aptitude Tests (DATS), AH2 and AH4. These tests do not give information of reading achievement relative to cognitive ability and academic potential.

For some of these tests timing is critical. Students are not meant to finish the test in the time allocated. The score is derived from how far they get through the test in the time allotted. In other tests the time is not so important. The allotted time is so generous that the majority of students will have answered all the questions with plenty of time to spare.

It is worth noting that The Public Appointments Service allows applicants with dyslexia additional time when taking standardised testing for recruitment and promotion purposes.

It may be difficult to get an accurate result on such tests for the student with dyslexia for the following reasons:

- Students may be slower in processing information. Here is an example based on the DATS (Differential Aptitude Testing). There is a generous time allowance for completing all but one section of the DATS. The majority of students finish the questions well within the time allotted. On the Numerical Reasoning section one student completed twenty-seven out of the forty questions consecutively and then ran out of time. All of their answers to that point were correct. It was obvious that with more time this student would have completed more questions and obtained a higher score. Their result is different to the student who has completed the full forty questions within the allotted time and got thirteen incorrect. Yet both students will be given the same result.

- These students may be slower in reading the instructions or in deciphering the sequence of instructions. This is critically important in Maths testing. Here is an example of a Maths question from a standardised test.

John spends three times as much as Michael on bus fares each week and Michael spends three times as much as Martin. If John spends 45p, how much does Martin spend?

For some students with dyslexia such a question is more a test of their English skills than their Maths abilities. They may need time to work out what the words mean and to interpret the sequence of instructions correctly. This makes their work much slower and sometimes they may not successfully decode what it is they are meant to do.

- They may lack the vocabulary to be able to do the task required. An example from another standardised test is as follows. It is a test of the student's ability to classify. They have to choose the odd one out from a series of words such as the following: *butcher, vicar, grocer, baker.* The students are given forty such problems and a limited amount of time in which to answer. No student is expected to complete the entire test. The score is based on how far they progress in the test. Lack of vocabulary and slowness in decoding the words on the page can slow down answering of students with dyslexia.

It is important that parents, students and teachers realise the limitations and unreliability of these tests for students with dyslexia and other learning difficulties. *They are not valid predictors of the student's ability*. For students with dyslexia the psychological assessment is a far more valid instrument for assessing their ability.

At primary level, no critical decisions are made based on standardised tests. However, the results could affect the child's self-image. Despite being told not to, students do compare the results achieved. Therefore it is important that the child understands the results are not reliable. Also, if teachers have not received training on the topic of learning difficulties, they also may form expectations of the child based on the results of standardised testing and not see the child's real potential. This is why it is so important that the psychological assessment report is brought into school and the student's profile with its strengths and weaknesses is discussed with the teacher.

Far more important is the fact that these tests may be used at entrance assessment at second level. Crucial decisions may be based on the student's performance in entrance assessment such as class placement and selection of options. Students who are placed in weaker classes due to a poor result in an entrance examination may find that taking subjects at higher level is not open to them. This will have major consequences later in second level and will affect results in both Junior and Leaving Certificate and, therefore, points in the CAO system.

Standardised tests of attainment for classroom use may be useful as base-line measures, for example at seven years of age, and as measures of progress made, for example at eleven years. They may identify teaching/learning targets met or not met but they present real difficulties for the learning disabled child. As not all low achievers are learning disabled, under this system there will continue to be the possibility of confusing dyslexic difficulties with low achievement. Therefore the importance of full psycho-educational assessment should not be underestimated.

4. Provision in the Irish School System

In this chapter you will read about the provision for students with dyslexia in the Irish school system. Such provision includes:

- Educational legislation;
- State agencies;
- Government publications;
- Additional teaching support;
- Other supports.

Educational Legislation

The Education Act 1998

Among the provisions of this Act are the following:

- The school shall provide education for students appropriate to their abilities and needs.
- The school shall use its available resources to ensure the educational needs of all students, including those with a disability or other special educational need, are identified and provided for.
- The Board of Management of the school shall publish … the policy of the school concerning admission to and participation in the school including the policy of the school relating to … admission to and participation by students with disabilities or who have other special educational needs and ensure that, as regards that policy, principles of equality and the right of parents to send their children to a school of the parents' choice are respected.
- The Board of Management shall make arrangements for the preparation of a school plan. This plan shall state the objectives of the school relating to equality of access to and participation in the school and the measures the school proposes to take to achieve those objectives including equality of access and participation in the school by students with disabilities or who have other special educational needs.

A grievance procedure is set out in the Act. It provides that the parent of a student or, in the case of a student who is 18, the student may appeal against the decision of a teacher or other member of staff of a school. It also provides an appeal procedure when a student is permanently excluded from school or a school refuses to enrol a student. The parents have the right to appeal to the Secretary General of the Department of Education and Science after they have been informed of the decisions by the school and have gone through any appeals procedure offered by the school.

The Education (Welfare) Act 2000

This Act safeguards every child's entitlement to an appropriate minimum education. It focuses particularly on causes of absenteeism. Included in its provisions are:

- The establishment of the National Educational Welfare Board, which has the lead role in implementing the Act. The Board deploys Educational Welfare Officers at local level who promote regular school attendance and prevent absenteeism and early school leaving. These officers focus in particular on children at risk who are experiencing difficulties in school with the purpose of resolving impediments to their regular attendance. Alternative schooling is sought for students who have been expelled, suspended or refused admittance to a school.
- School managers have the responsibility of adopting a proactive approach to school attendance by maintaining a register of students and notifying the Educational Welfare Officer of particular problems in relation to attendance. They should also prepare and implement a school attendance strategy to encourage regular school attendance.
- The Act makes specific provision for the continuing education and training of young persons aged sixteen and seventeen years who leave school early to take up employment.
- The central role of parents in providing for their child's education is recognised. Parents should send their children to school on each school day or otherwise ensure they are receiving an appropriate minimum education. If the child is absent, the parents should notify the school principal of the reason for the absence.

The Education of Persons with Special Educational Needs Act 2004

This Act provides for the inclusive education for the child with special educational needs (SEN) in mainstream schooling. It defines a child with SEN as one who learns differently. This definition positively includes children with dyslexia. The Act set up the National Council for Special Education. Among the duties of the Council are the following:

- To communicate to schools and parents information on best practice concerning the education of children with SEN;
- To plan and co-ordinate provision for the education and support services for children with SEN;
- To assess and review resources required for the educational provision for children with SEN.

The Council employs Special Educational Needs Organisers (SENOs) who give advice and assistance to schools. They have a

role in planning an individual education plar
with SEN in collaboration with the teache
child. They decide on applications fr/
resources for students with SEN.

The Act sets out that if the principal of
that a student is not benefiting from the
provided in the school and that these diᵤᵤ
cial educational need, the principal, in consultatiᵤᵢ .
ents, shall arrange for an assessment of the student as souᵢ.
possible and not later than one month.

If the assessment establishes that the student has special educational needs, the principal, within one month of receipt of the assessment, will ensure an education plan for the student is drawn up. The
contents of such a plan are specified in the Act. The principal should
give parents and the SENO a copy of the plan.

The Council has the power to designate the school that a child
with SEN is to attend and that school shall admit the child on being
so directed by the Council. In making such a designation the
Council has to take into account the needs of the child, the
wishes of the child's parents and the capacity of the school to
accommodate the child and meet their needs.

The Act contains an appeals procedure for parents if they
believe the special educational needs of their child are not being
addressed.

State Agencies

National Educational Psychological Service (NEPS)

The National Educational Psychological Service (NEPS) was
established in 1999 and is an executive agency of the Department
of Education and Science. The development plan for NEPS provides for the gradual expansion over a period of years, with the
number of psychologists increasing to two hundred.

NEPS has been delegated authority to develop and provide an
educational psychological service to all students in primary and
post-primary schools and in certain other centres supported by the
Department. NEPS provides the following services to schools:

- Consultation and casework about individual students;
- Work of a more preventive or developmental nature.

chologist is responsible for a number of schools. The authorities provide names of children who are giving cause oncern and discuss the relative urgency of each case during psychologist's visit. This allows the psychologist to give priority urgent cases. Where cases are less urgent, the psychologist, as a preliminary measure, acts as a consultant to teachers and parents, and offers advice about educational/behavioural plans and monitors progress. The psychologist is also involved in assessing students for reasonable accommodation in state examinations.

Until NEPS becomes fully staffed, there will be a backlog of assessments. Priority is given to those students in greatest need. As a result, there may be waiting lists. Consequently many parents opt for private assessments. Tax relief was introduced on the fees paid on private assessments. This is claimed by using the MED 1 form. The NEPS website is found on the Department of Education and Science website www.education.ie.

Special Education Support Service (SESS)

This service was set up in 2003. The aim of the service is to enhance the quality of teaching and learning with particular reference to the education of children with special needs. It is targeted at teachers in mainstream primary and post-primary schools as well as special schools.

SESS provides this service through the following initiatives:

- It provides teachers with professional development. An example of such support is subsidising the cost of on-line courses offered by Prof-excel on topics such as dyslexia, ADHD, autism and inclusion;
- The provision of in-service training on special education topics;
- Telephone and on-line query service;
- Local Initiative Schemes, where schools can apply for assistance to meet their needs on special education. This assistance may be financial, professional or advisory.

The SESS website (www.sess.ie) is comprehensive, offering information on categories of special needs, resources available, courses available, latest developments in special education and quick reference to official documents such as Department of Education and Science circulars and legislation on the topic of Special Education.

National Council for Special Education (NCSE)

The National Council for Special Education (NCSE) was set up under the Education of Persons with Special Education Needs Act 2004. The details of the work of the Council were outlined at the beginning of this chapter in the section on the Education of Persons with Special Educational Needs Act.

Government Publications

Report of the Task Force on Dyslexia

In 2000 a Task Force on Dyslexia was set up whose brief was to examine the current range of educational provision and support services available to children with specific reading disabilities in Ireland, to assess the adequacy of current educational provision and support services and to make recommendations for the development of policy approaches, educational provision and support services.

The report was completed in 2001 and published on the government website at www.education.ie. The Task Force looked for submissions from the public and received 399 written submissions. The Task Force also decided to look for oral submissions from the public. This recognised the fact that some individuals with dyslexia would find it easier to make an oral submission than a written one. Adverts quoting a free telephone number were made on the radio. As a result 896 oral submissions were received.

The Task Force gave a definition of dyslexia that recognised the broad range of difficulties which arise from the condition and that also took into account recent research findings. It is a common misperception of dyslexia that it has to do only with reading and spelling and so this definition is very useful as it acknowledges the wide range of difficulties that may be present.

A welcome statement in the report is that 'each student with learning difficulties arising from dyslexia should receive a level of provision appropriate to his/her needs'. The Task Force recommended that since the difficulties presented by students with dyslexia range along a continuum from mild to severe, there is a need for a continuum of interventions and other services.

The Task Force suggested a scheme that would involve class teacher, learning support teacher and parents working in co-operation to support the child. The role and contribution of parents is emphasised throughout the report.

The first recommendation of the report was that appropriate printed and electronic material on dyslexia be distributed to all schools. This has resulted in the publication of the video/CD ROM/DVD *Understanding Dyslexia*.

Understanding Dyslexia video/CD ROM/DVD

This video/CD ROM/DVD is a joint initiative of the Departments of Education in Ireland, North and South, and was issued to all schools in 2005.

- The video has eight sections and features professionals, parents, students and adults with dyslexia. This is a very good introduction to the subject of dyslexia in Ireland. Topics covered include the signs and facts about dyslexia, recognition of dyslexia, interventions and how parents and teachers can help.
- The CD ROM is a comprehensive and invaluable resource for teachers and other professionals dealing with dyslexia. The contents are too extensive to list here, but to give some idea the following are included:
  - The Task Force Report;
  - A discussion on the definition of dyslexia;
  - Advice and strategies for teachers, both primary and post-primary, and for parents. These can be downloaded as booklets;
  - A self-help section for the pupil;
  - Comprehensive listing of resources such as books, websites, tests and teaching materials.
- The DVD includes both the video and the information on the CD ROM.

Learning Support Guidelines

The Learning Support Guidelines were published by the Department of Education and Science in 2000. The primary purpose of these guidelines is to provide practical guidance to teachers and parents on the provision of effective learning support to pupils with low achievement/learning difficulties. The guidelines address the following topics:

- The principles of good practice in the provision of learning support in schools;
- The need for a policy statement on the provision of learning support in the context of a whole-school plan;

- The adoption of a collaborative approach by those involved including the principal teacher, class teachers, the learning support teacher and the parents;
- Screening and identification of pupils, selection of pupils for supplementary teaching and evaluation of the progress of the pupil at the end of each term;
- Details of the individual profile and learning programme that should be drawn up for each pupil receiving additional help.

Additional Teaching Support

The Department of Education and Science provides additional teaching support for students with dyslexia in three different ways:

1. Extra teaching support through the provision of learning support or resource teaching;
2. Special classes attached to a mainstream school;
3. Special schools for children with specific learning difficulties.

This support is targeted at those students in greatest need as defined by the Department of Education and Science criteria. As a result not all students with dyslexia qualify for such support. The Report of the Task Force on Dyslexia described dyslexia as occurring in a continuum from mild to severe. It recommended the adoption of a model of provision based on meeting the needs for each student. A continuum of interventions should be available to students matched to the severity and persistence of their learning difficulties.

Extra teaching support

The terms resource, learning support and remedial have been used to describe additional teaching support provided for children. Increasingly the term special needs teacher is being used, which describes both learning support and resource teaching.

Resource teaching is granted based on an individual application for a child with special educational needs to the SENO for the school. Such applications have to be accompanied by relevant psycho-educational/medical reports.

Learning support teaching is provided to children with low achievement. It was formerly called remedial teaching. It does not need an individual application. Assessment for access to such help is done in school through the use of standardised testing. The Learning Support Guidelines state that when selecting pupils for such help, priority should be given to those who achieve scores that are at or below the 10th percentile on a standardised test of English reading or mathematics.

The Department of Education and Science Circulars SP ED 01/05 and SP ED 09/04 set out new arrangements for the allocation of special education resources at primary level. In May 2005 the Minister for Education and Science, Mary Hanafin, announced further changes in the allocation of these resources. A weighted allocation has been introduced to cater for pupils with higher incidence special educational needs and those with learning support needs, i.e. those functioning at or below the 10th percentile on a standardised test of reading and/or mathematics. The circular states the higher incidence special educational needs are borderline mild general disability, mild general learning disability and specific learning difficulty.

The weighted system meant that special needs teaching posts are granted on the following basis:

- In all-boy schools the first special education teaching post at 135 pupils, a second post at 295 and so on;
- In mixed schools one post for 145 pupils, a second post at 315 pupils and so on;
- In all-girl schools the first post at 195 pupils, the second at 395 pupils and so on;
- In disadvantaged schools the first post at 80 pupils, the second at 160 pupils and so on;
- There was also increased provision made for smaller schools.

There are children in the higher incidence group in the education system at the present time that have been granted individual allocations. These allocations will continue for these students until they leave the school.

In addition there are specific allocations in respect of pupils with low incidence disabilities. The low incidence disabilities include physical impairment, hearing impairment, visual impairment, emotional disturbance, severe emotional disturbance, autism, autistic spectrum difficulties, moderate general learning disability and specific speech and language disorder. Applications for these pupils are made on an individual basis to the SENO.

This new model of provision means that there are more special needs teachers in the schools. It also means that, in the future, the child with dyslexia will be covered by the general allocation to the school. There will not be individual allocations to children with higher incidence special educational needs. A new circular SP ED 02/05 was issued in September 2005, which gives further clarification on the organisation of teaching resources for pupils who need additional support at primary level.

This new system is designed to put resources permanently in place in schools and therefore facilitate early and flexible intervention. It allows better planning, as schools know the resources available. One of the advantages of this model is stated in the Department of Education press release to be that it will reduce the need for individual applications and therefore the need for assessments to support such applications. While teachers may have well-founded suspicions that a student has dyslexia, an assessment is required for a diagnosis to be made. It is not clear whether this means that fewer children will be referred for assessment. This could result in the child getting extra teaching support, but the reasons why such help is required will not be investigated. In order to provide the most effective intervention, it is necessary to understand the causes of the difficulties. A child with mild general learning difficulty requires different teaching strategies to those required by a child with dyslexia. Assessments are still necessary when applying for supports such as an exemption from Irish, reasonable accommodation in exams or access to the support services at third level.

At second level, Circular PPT 01/05 advises school authorities of the establishment of the National Council for Special Education. It also refers to three other circulars: M 08/99, SP ED 07/02 and SP ED 08/02. These circulars form the basis for determining if a child has a special educational need and what extra teaching or other supports should be put in place. Circular SP ED 08/02 states that for students to qualify for resource teaching under the heading specific learning difficulty, they must have been assessed by a psychologist as:

- Being of average intelligence or higher;
- Having a degree of learning disability specific to the basic skills in reading, writing or mathematics that places them at or below the 2nd percentile on suitable, standardised, norm-referenced tests.

Application for resource hours is made in February. Parents of students entering second level should ensure that the school has psychological reports by this stage if an application for resource teaching is to be made. It means that, in the case of students for whom resource teaching is appropriate, the school can apply to the SENO for the necessary resource allocation and have it in place by the September of entry.

The learning support teacher provides learning support to children with low achievement. The Learning Support Guidelines set out that supplementary teaching should be provided to students who have not yet achieved basic competence in English and Mathematics, i.e. those performing below the 10th percentile on nationally standardised tests of literacy and numeracy.

These criteria for resource and learning support mean that students with dyslexia whose scores are higher than the 2nd or 10th percentile respectively do not fall within the criteria for additional teaching support.

This is an area of rapid change in education. The Department of Education and Science website (www.education.ie) and the SESS website (www.sess.ie) provide access to circulars for those who want to follow the ongoing developments in the provision of extra support for students.

Education plans

Under the Education of Persons with Special Educational Needs Act, an individual education plan (IEP) should be drawn up for the child who has been assessed as having special educational needs. For the child who falls within the criteria for learning support an individual profile and learning programme (IPLP) is drawn up. Both are very similar and record information about learning attainments and learning strengths of the student. Both contain an outline of the learning programme that sets out learning targets and activities. The learning support/resource/special needs teachers have a key role in such planning. However, it is strongly recommended that an inclusive approach involving class teacher(s), parents and students themselves be adopted in both the diagnostic and planning stages and later in implementation and monitoring of such plans.

Special classes attached to mainstream schools

Special classes (units) for children with specific learning difficulties (including those arising from dyslexia) have been established in designated schools where there are a sufficient number of students with such difficulties to form a class. The pupil-teacher ratio for these classes is 9:1. Students are placed in the classes for one or two years and then they return to mainstream classes. There are nineteen such units throughout the country. The Department of Education and Science website gives details of locations.

The criteria for access to such special classes, which are set out in the Department of Education and Science document Revised Guidelines for the Enrolment of Children with Specific Learning Difficulty (June 1998), are as follows:

> Assessment by a psychologist on a standardised test of intelligence should place general intellectual ability within the average range or above ... There must be an obvious discrepancy between general intellectual ability and performance on a standardised test of reading ability ... It would be expected that not more than two per cent of the overall student population would be found in this category. Performance in basic literacy skills as measured by a standardised test should be at a very low level compared to the vast majority of students in a similar age cohort. Consideration should also be given to the child's speaking, writing and spelling skills as well as to his/her level of adaptation to learning within mainstream education, to his/her progress in other aspects of the curriculum and to his/her social and personal development ... Students transferring to a special school or support unit for students with specific learning difficulties should have completed second class in a primary school or be at least eight years old on the first day of the school year.

Special schools for children with specific learning difficulties

The Department of Education and Science has established four primary schools for students with specific learning difficulties including those arising from dyslexia. These schools are as follows:

- St Killian's, Bishopstown, Cork;
- St Oliver Plunkett's, Monkstown, Co. Dublin;
- Catherine McAuley's, 59 Lower Baggot Street, Dublin 2;
- St Rose's, Balrothery, Tallaght, Dublin 24.

The criteria for access to these schools are similar to those for access to special classes.

Support for students who do not qualify for additional teaching

Some students with dyslexia do not meet the criteria set by the Department of Education for access to extra teaching supports such as learning support/resource teaching or special classes or schools. However, they may still experience varying degrees of difficulty in school. The Report of the Task Force on Dyslexia recognised that since the difficulties presented by students with dyslexia range along a continuum from mild to severe, there is a need for a continuum of interventions and other services. Some students with mild dyslexia may need minimal intervention and yet this intervention is essential if the student is to reach full potential and achievement. An example from second level is the student who may only need a waiver of spelling and grammar in the state examinations and that teachers are informed of the presence of dyslexia. If the student does not fall within the learning support/resource remit, whose responsibility is it to ensure that such interventions are in place? Whole-school planning should clearly set out the roles and responsibilities of the staff involved.

The Report of the Task Force stressed the key role of the class/subject teacher in providing support. Even if students are receiving learning support/resource teaching, they spend the majority of the school day with the mainstream teacher. The student who receives no additional teaching relies totally on the class/subject teacher. For this reason it is vital that all teachers receive pre-service and in-service training on the topic of dyslexia.

The Dyslexia Association of Ireland (DAI) workshop classes and exam preparation classes provide an example of the targeted help that can be provided for such students. These workshops are run throughout the country. Details of the workshops are available on the DAI website (www.dyslexia.ie).

Other Supports

Exemption from Irish

Irish is a compulsory subject for students in primary and post-primary schools. However, students with specific learning difficulties including those arising from dyslexia may be granted an exemption from the study of Irish. Such an exemption is given to students who function intellectually at average or above-average level but have a specific learning difficulty of such a degree of severity that they fail to achieve expected levels of attainment in basic language skills in the mother tongue. The guideline for such exemptions is that the student is achieving at or below the 10th percentile on a standardised norm-referenced test of reading or spelling. Circular M10/94 sets out the details regarding the exemption from Irish. In August 2005, there were media reports that a new circular on Irish exemptions was being prepared for publication by the Department of Education and Science.

The procedure for gaining an exemption involves the parent submitting a written application on behalf of the child to the school principal along with a copy of a report from a psycho-educational assessment that is less than two years old and which recommends that the student should be exempt because the criteria are met. If the school authorities grant an exemption, a certificate is issued and the Department of Education and Science is informed. The exemption granted at primary level will be recognised at second level and for entry to the National University of Ireland (NUI) colleges. The exemption should be taken into account at entrance assessment when students are transferring to second-level if Irish is included as part of the assessment.

Students who attend the special schools referred to in the previous section of this chapter may apply for an exemption from Irish when leaving these schools.

Some students may fall within the guideline of the 10th percentile at one stage, but with additional tuition, may develop their skills in English. Therefore at one stage they may qualify for such an exemption and, if assessed at a later stage, may not. If the student qualifies for the exemption at a particular point in time, it would be prudent to get the official certificate. Parents may decide to let the student continue to participate in Irish class in order to benefit from the cultural aspects of the subject. By having the official certificate they then have the option further on in the educational system to withdraw the student from Irish. This could be of major benefit to senior-cycle students who intend to apply to the Central Applications Office (CAO). Entry to CAO colleges is determined by points. Senior-cycle students should be able to present their best subjects for examination to maximise points and be able to compete on equal terms.

Take the case of a student in 2004 with very good Maths and technical ability but poorer verbal abilities who applied for an Engineering degree in one of the National University of Ireland (NUI) colleges. The entry requirements for NUI colleges state that students must have English, Irish and a third language. This student began his Leaving Certificate course taking nine subjects. He did not qualify for an Irish exemption as he was outside the 10th percentile. He was studying English, Irish and French at ordinary level due to weaker verbal skills. He then had to take six other subjects at higher level in order to maximise his points. His higher level subjects were Maths, Applied Maths, Physics, Geography, Technical Graphics and Accounting. Most Leaving Certificate students do seven subjects. This student, who has a learning difficulty, was in the position of having to take two additional subjects outside school time. He applied for and received an exemption from the NUI third-language requirement in the course of fifth year. This reduced the number of his subjects to eight. He achieved 475 points based on his six higher level subjects. He therefore got a place on his chosen course. If he did not have two additional subjects he would have received 365 points, a difference of 110 points. Many students with dyslexia have a similar profile of ability and could face the same difficulties in maximising their performance in the very competitive points race that exists for places in the CAO system.

There are some careers where a certain standard of Irish is required. A 'C' in higher level Irish in the Leaving Certificate is necessary for primary teaching. It affects a small number of career choices if the student does not study Irish. At time of going to press it is still a requirement for entry to the Gardaí. Applicants require a minimum of a 'C' grade at foundation level. In December 2004 the Minister for Justice indicated there might be a review of this requirement.

Sometimes a teacher at primary level, recognising a child's difficulties, allows the child to do extra English work during the allocated time for Irish. However, the official exemption is not issued. If the student is not studying Irish at primary level, it is very important for a parent to ask the school for the certificate of exemption. Otherwise the child will be required to study Irish when attending second-level.

If the student is exempt from Irish, there should be provision for this class time to be used constructively such as learning support withdrawal, additional English reading or computer time.

Exemption from the NUI third-language requirement

The National University of Ireland (NUI) comprises the colleges of UCC, UCD, UCG and Maynooth. The entry requirements for NUI colleges specify that a student must pass six subjects in the Leaving Certificate, two at higher level, and that the student must include English, Irish and a third language.

NUI recognises the exemption from Irish granted at primary or post-primary and also allows a student with such an exemption to be exempt from the third-language requirement for entry to NUI. This means that students do not have to take Irish and a third language as subjects in the Leaving Certificate. It is important to apply to NUI, preferably during fifth year, for recognition of the Irish exemption and to apply for the third-language exemption.

If students are not exempt from Irish, they may still qualify for an exemption from the third-language requirement. NUI considers applications for such an exemption from students who are certified by a qualified professional as having a serious dyslexic condition. The application should be made prior to entry to senior cycle at second level, before subject choice for the Leaving Certificate has been made. Forms are available from NUI at 49 Merrion Square, Dublin 2.

It is vital when applying to the CAO that information about such exemptions is provided and that it is mentioned on the statement of application that each applicant receives in April/May from the CAO.

Special arrangements/reasonable accommodations in state examinations

Reasonable accommodation is the phrase used to describe the various types of support provided for students in the state examinations. The types of help include:

- *Extra time to be given for the examination.* An additional twenty minutes is given for each examination session in the subjects Irish, English, History, Economic History and Geography in the Leaving Certificate examination. All students taking the examination can avail of this time. Other than this provision, extra time is not granted to students with dyslexia.
- *Reading assistance.* A reader should only be granted where a candidate is unable to read the paper. This means the candidate must have a severe reading difficulty and that in the absence of the assistance of a reader the candidate would be unable to take the examination. The explanatory note on the certificate and statement of results will read, 'All parts of the examination in this subject were examined except the reading element'.
- *Tape recorder or computer.* The use of a tape recorder or computer is appropriate where it can be established that the candidate has good oral ability, good knowledge of the course content, a score well below average on a spelling test and more than 20 per cent of the target words unrecognisable under test and on written samples. The explanatory note on the English result will read, 'all parts of the examination in this subject were assessed except spelling and written punctuation elements'. In the other language subjects it will read, 'all parts of the examination in this subject were assessed except for the spelling and some grammatical elements'.

- *A waiver from the spelling and grammatical components in language subjects.* This exemption is considered appropriate where it can be established that the candidate has good oral ability, good knowledge of the course content, a score well below average on a spelling test and that the target word is easily recognisable as the target word, although mis-spelt. The explanatory note is similar to that for the tape recorder or computer.

Students who are given the accommodation of taping, use of reader or use of word processor take the examinations in a centre by themselves with a supervisor. Students who have been granted the accommodation of a waiver from spelling and grammar take the examination in the main examination centre.

Applications for reasonable accommodation are made by the school. The school sends the application form for accommodations at Leaving Certificate level to the Department of Education and Science and includes a psychological report and samples of the student's work. Parents must sign this form. Applications for accommodations in the Leaving Certificate are made in late May for the following year. It is important that the applications are in by the due date. The application is processed through NEPS. The NEPS psychologist comes to the school to interview the student and staff. In some cases additional testing may be carried out. The psychologist decides if the accommodation is granted. If an application is turned down, there is an appeals procedure.

For the Junior Certificate, applications are made in October/November prior to the exam. For Junior Certificate students, there is a less rigorous application process. The form is simpler and there is no need for an assessment to accompany the application. Accommodations are usually granted if the school applies for them.

Approximately 116,000 students sit state examinations annually.

Table 4.1: Numbers granted reasonable accommodations in 2005

	Leaving Cert.	Junior Cert.
Reader	656	2356
Tape	194	606
Word processor	41	50
Waiver spelling and grammar	1396	3367

It is important that there is an objective assessment by the school of which reasonable accommodations, if any, would be appropriate for a particular student. Sometimes parents may be looking for any possible help and yet such help might not be appropriate or helpful to the student. Ways to help determine what accommodations are appropriate can include:

- Teachers correct house exam scripts in language subjects twice. In the first correction they include the marks for spelling and grammar. They then re-mark the script excluding these marks to see if there is a significant difference in overall grade obtained.
- The student is asked to prepare for a test on a particular topic. An exam on this material can be given in traditional format and then by using a tape, word processor or a reader. Again the purpose would be to look for a significant difference in marks obtained.

If the use of a word processor might be appropriate, a preliminary step is the development of excellent keyboarding skills early on at second level. Otherwise it is not possible to ascertain if the use of the word processor would be of benefit.

If a particular form of reasonable accommodation is considered appropriate, such accommodation should be given in the house exams in the school. Indeed it is essential that the mock exams prior to the state exam be taken using the accommodation granted. This is very demanding on school resources to provide such accommodations as it may mean that a teacher has to be freed to supervise such exam students on a one-to-one basis. Very often the necessary number of staff may not be available. It may be possible to use parental assistance to help out or to train transition year students to act as readers or supervisors of the taping of the exams.

The student will also need training in the use of the accommodation granted. It may be a stressful experience to take an examination alone with an adult present. Repeated practice can reduce this stress. The student also needs to know the role of the supervisor and the help that can be given. In reading aloud the supervisor can only read what is on the paper, but the student can request particular sections to be reread as often as needed.

When using a tape recorder, the student needs practice in giving the exact details such as the number and section of the question being answered. Taped answers may be too short, possibly because it is difficult to check over what has already been said, whereas with a written answer it is possible to scan the answer quickly. The student can use some blank paper to help structure the answer by making a list of the points to be included before speaking to the tape. The student should also ensure that the tape recorder is turned off when it is not being used. It is also important to start the taping session by checking that the tape recorder is recording clearly and that the answers are audible.

Another reason for short answers may be because of embarrassment in the one-to-one situation with the supervisor. The school appoints the supervisor for exams taken with a reader or taping and it can be someone with whom the student is familiar. This may reduce the embarrassment.

In the case of the reasonable accommodations of reading assistance, use of a tape or word processor, the student is in a special exam centre within the student's school. The fact that the student is separated from the rest of the student body during the exams is a very public statement. This is at a time of development in adolescence when many young people want to be part of the peer group and do not want to be considered different. As a result some students may be reluctant to use such accommodations. However, when it is made evident to them the difference in grades they may achieve, it might help them to overcome their initial reluctance.

The introduction of the explanatory note on the certificate is a cause of concern to the Dyslexia Association of Ireland (DAI) and to parents. It is a permanent statement on the certificate of the student. For future employers, who may not be familiar with dyslexia and its effects, the wording of the different explanatory notes might imply the student cannot read, spell or use grammar at all. This is more important for the student who opts for employment directly after second level. There is no such explanatory note on the certificates, diplomas and degrees issued by third-level colleges and PLC courses and, in all probability, employers will not ask to see the Junior or Leaving Certificates of applicants with further qualifications.

The examiners of scripts in the state examinations are second-level teachers. Many teachers have not received formal training in how dyslexia presents in written work in either pre-service or in-service training. As a result they may not be aware of how bizarre the phonic spelling of some students with dyslexia can be. Correcting exam papers for students with dyslexia takes more time than the usual. Poor handwriting, unusual spellings and poorly expressed facts can mean the teacher has to decipher the script to see if the student has the correct answers. If examiners do not have experience of dyslexic scripts, it is quite possible that the student may lose marks. Such a concern is noted in the Report of the

Task Force on Dyslexia.

The DAI has requested the State Examinations Commission to include such training in the conferences that are held in June when examiners receive guidelines on the correction of scripts in state examinations until the time comes when all post-primary teachers have received adequate training.

Grants for the purchase of equipment

There is a scheme for the purchase of equipment for pupils with a disability. It applies to pupils who have been diagnosed as having serious physical and/or communicative disabilities of a degree that makes ordinary communication through speech and/or writing impossible for them. The purpose of the scheme is to provide the pupils with equipment that is deemed necessary and of direct educational benefit to them. Examples of such equipment include computers, tape-recorders and word processors. The application is made by the school to the SENO and must be accompanied by a comprehensive professional assessment.

5. Dyslexia: The Early Years

This chapter will be of most use to parents. In it you will read about:

- Early signs of dyslexia;
- Screening tests for young children;
- Developing the skills necessary for reading;
- Helping the young child with social skills.

There is a certain 'Catch 22' element about early identification of dyslexia. All experts agree that the earlier the difficulty is identified and remediation begun, the more likely it is that the child will cope with school and learning. However, as dyslexia shows itself most clearly as a reading difficulty, it is not usually suspected until the child has tried and failed to learn to read. By that time the child may be seven or older. Much valuable learning time will have been lost and the child's confidence in their ability will probably have been damaged. So the question arises, how do you identify a reading difficulty in a child who has not yet been taught to read? And should we put so much emphasis on learning to read at an early age?

Early identification is, undoubtedly, very important for children with dyslexia but one has to beware of making a premature diagnosis. Children develop at very different rates and while one child is ready to read at age four, another may not be ready until much later. Most Irish children start formal schooling at age four and teaching of reading commences soon after. In many countries reading is not taught until age six or even seven. Studies show that these children have caught up with Irish children by age nine. So we must ask – are we putting too much emphasis on early teaching of reading? There are many other skills that children must learn first. Can we say definitively that a child has a dyslexic-type reading difficulty rather than simply being on a different developmental timescale to other children of a similar age?

Early Signs of Dyslexia

While reading difficulty may be the most obvious sign of dyslexia, there are other more subtle indicators. Many parents worry that because their five or six year old reverses letters or writes some numbers backwards they have dyslexia. Happily, this does not usually indicate a problem. Most children do this until the age of seven or even later. One sign does not mean a child has dyslexia. There are a number of indicators and, unless a child checks positive for several items on the list, no further action is needed.

> It is the severity of the trait, the clarity with which it may be observed, and the length of time during which it persists which give the vital clues to the identification of the dyslexic learner.
> (Augur, 1997: 57)

Below is a list of possible indicators of a dyslexic difficulty. (See also the indicators listed in the Report of the Task Force in Chapter 2.)

- Delay in the development of speech and language;
- Problems with naming (i.e. mislabelling);
- Difficulty in doing simple jigsaws;
- Difficulty in copying shapes with pencil;
- Difficulty in colouring pictures within the lines;
- Difficulty with simple sequences such as days of the week;
- Difficulty in identifying and remembering rhymes;
- Enjoys being read to, but shows no desire to learn to read;
- Inability to remember the order of simple instructions;
- Clumsiness, poor co-ordination, trips up and bumps into things;
- Difficulties getting dressed, fastening buttons, tying laces, putting shoes on the correct feet;
- Poor concentration, easy distractibility and does not seem to listen;
- Delay in establishing dominant hand, eye and foot;
- Family history of dyslexia or specific learning problems.

If a consistent pattern of the above difficulties emerges, then positive actions should be taken. Children do not 'grow out' of dyslexia. It will not go away if ignored. Some professional advice may be necessary, either in the area of language development, dyslexia screening or full psycho-educational assessment.

Speech and language

The presence of an early speech and language difficulty should alert parents to the possible existence of other difficulties. Before reading even begins, language development must take place. If a child has difficulty in understanding spoken language, there is a risk of written language difficulty. A professional assessment may be necessary to determine the cause of the problem. Factors such as hearing loss, general developmental delay, social, cultural or emotional problems need to be investigated. If a specific speech and/or language delay is diagnosed then speech therapy may be necessary before reading or spelling can be taught successfully.

Speech and language assessment is provided by the Health Boards and referral is normally through the family doctor or the school. As there is great demand on this service parents may opt to seek private assessment. The Irish Association of Speech and Language Therapists can supply names of qualified therapists.

Visual perception

Often children have some delay in visual perceptual development. While children's visual acuity is checked out in the school, there may be more subtle features of perception that are not revealed by these tests. Children with poor spatial awareness, clumsiness and poor hand–eye co-ordination may be experiencing difficulty with visual rather than motor functioning. Many children confuse directions of letters and numbers and are slow to read consistently from left to right. These difficulties may be evident in a dislike for making jigsaws, colouring within lines or catching balls. Visual perceptual delay is not necessarily an indication of dyslexia but may be implicated. Persistent visual perceptual difficulties may need to be examined by an optometrist.

Screening Tests for Young Children

If parents or teachers find cause for concern in younger children, there are some screening tests that can be given to children as young as four. These screening tests can be used to decide if a child needs a full psycho-educational assessment from a psychologist. They can also be useful in providing information about the child's learning strengths and weaknesses, and in devising an individual education programme. Such tests usually include diagnostic tests and attainment tests. Diagnostic tests examine how the child performs on tasks that are known to be affected by dyslexia and the attainment tests look at how the child has assimilated what has been taught to date.

Probably one of the most widely used tests is the Dyslexia Early Screening Test (DEST), devised by Dr Rod Nicholson and Dr Angela Fawcett of Sheffield University. It is one of a series of three tests that can be used from early childhood to adult screening. The DEST is intended for children between the ages of four-and-a-half and six-and-a-half. The advantage is that it can be given by the class or special needs teacher. It is available from ETC Consult in Dublin.

Computerised programmes are also available as another screening device. An example of such tests is Lucid CoPS

(Cognitive Profiling System), which can be given to children between the ages of four and eight. This is a fully computerised programme that teachers can administer. It includes nine tests that are said to predict dyslexic-type difficulties. It provides teachers with a profile of the learner that can assist in the preparation of the individual pupil learning profile. It is available from Edtech Software Ltd in Co. Mayo.

An early screening test based on Irish data and geared to the Irish educational system is being piloted in 2005 in over 200 primary schools. This work is being done through the Psychology Department in Trinity College, Dublin.

Definitive assessment of dyslexia by a suitably qualified psychologist is not usually obtained until the age of seven or older. This means that a child may be attending school for three years before full diagnosis is reached. Early screening may make parents and teachers aware of potential difficulties and so enable them to use the child's early school years to the best advantage. Many parents, particularly those with a family history of dyslexia, have a shrewd idea that a potential difficulty exists even before a screening test is carried out.

Developing the Skills Necessary for Reading

So what can parents and teachers do to help a child with dyslexia before a formal diagnosis has been made? There are many activities that can help a child to develop important pre-reading and other skills. Some of these activities are outlined below but many parents and teachers devise their own. This list offers a variety from which parents and/or teachers can pick and choose. It would not be possible to attempt all of these activities. The most important thing is for parents and children to find something that they enjoy and that does not put pressure on child or adult. Children enjoy activities that challenge them a little, particularly when parents, childminders, grandparents or friends are involved. These activities benefit any child, whether or not dyslexic tendencies exist. They may take a little time and organisation but they do not require special equipment or expertise and can be carried out at any time and in any place. In this regard grandparents are often a wonderful resource: they may have more free time than other adults in the child's life and they can offer a great deal simply from their own life experience.

General activities

- Talking to children is something we all take for granted. However, the words and range of vocabulary used, the ideas expressed and the tone of voice all contribute not only to their understanding of language and communication but also to their feeling of self-esteem.
- Listening to a child is equally important. A child with dyslexic difficulties may well have some expressive language problems and may take a long time to tell a story or may get the order of events confused. A busy parent could be tempted to hurry the child or to finish sentences, but encouraging the child to tell a story in sequence and to give all the relevant information develops vital language skills.
- Saying nursery rhymes together is a great way to improve vocabulary and develop an awareness of rhythm and rhyme.
- Games involving mime and drama develop the child's visual skills.
- Games and songs where the child has to follow instructions, such as *Simon Says* or the *Hokey Cokey*, help a child to follow instructions and learn that certain things have to be done in sequence.
- Television can be a very stimulating and entertaining medium if used intelligently. There are some excellent programmes that can be watched together and discussed. If a parent watches a programme with a child and shows interest in it, this makes it more important in the child's eyes and more likely to be remembered. Even quite young children can be interested in news events of the day and they benefit from discussion and explanation of what is happening in the world.
- Introduce children to computers as soon as they are ready. There are now many early learning computer programmes designed for pre-school children. These provide a fun way to learn as well as introducing children to computers.
- Finally, the old games that develop hand–eye co-ordination and develop motor skills should not be forgotten. Many children with dyslexia tend to be clumsy and may not perform as well as their peers at games. Parents can help greatly by encouraging the child to master activities such as cycling, roller skating and skipping in a non-competitive environment. It is very important to the child's self-esteem to be able to do these activities but it may take longer to acquire the skill. Parents can help by encouraging perseverance and teaching that all skills improve with practice.

Some of the following activities may be more familiar to the pre-school or infant class teachers but there is no reason why parents should not try some of them. The most important thing is for these activities to be presented in a relaxed setting and that the child does not see them as a chore or, worse still, another task at which they may fail.

Listening (auditory) activities

- With eyes closed, try to get the child to identify everyday sounds such as the clock ticking or traffic going by.
- Tape everyday sounds and play a game where the child has to identify the sounds.
- With eyes closed, try to get the child to recognise the speaker from the voice.
- Clapping out syllables in words or tapping out the rhythm in a poem develop auditory awareness.
- Songs like *Old McDonald* and *Ten Green Bottles* involve memory and sequencing.

Looking (visual) activities

- Play card games like *Snap* and *Pairs* with both pictures and symbols, and then move on to using letters and words. It is important to avoid the competitive element in games, so playing with an adult rather than a peer can be helpful. Nothing deflates a child's self-esteem more than having a younger sibling out-perform them.
- Sorting pictures by colour, shape and size helps develop aware-ness of the visual appearance of objects. This concept is useful when reading, as the shape and length of a word can be useful clues.
- Get the child to look at a picture and remember all the details they can. Then cover it and ask questions about it.
- Provide a tray with several objects on it. Give the child a few minutes to study what is on it. Then take it away and ask them to name what was on the tray.
- Draw basic shapes on cards. Lay out a series of these cards and ask the child to remember the sequence and then draw it. Gradu-ally increase the length of the sequence.
- Cut up basic cartoon strips and mix them up. Then ask the child to rearrange the parts to recreate the story.

- Provide several pictures and ask the child to create a story around them.
- Play *Odd One Out* games with pictures or objects such as an onion, carrot, orange and potato.

Kinaesthetic awareness

- Encourage the child to trace shapes, letters and words.
- Make letters and words with pipe cleaners or play dough.
- Make letter shapes and words on a rough material such as sand, carpet, sandpaper or even on the child's palm.
- Feel and name wooden or plastic shapes or letters with eyes closed.
- Jigsaw puzzles are very important.

Co-ordination and balance

- Don't forget about physical skills. Throwing, catching, skipping, hopping, jumping and balancing are all important skills to master. Some children will need to practice these skills consciously. The little skills, which many children acquire naturally, may have to be taught to children with dyslexia.

Introducing books

- An early introduction to books is an advantage to any child. It is important to read to children, to talk about the story, to look at pictures and ask the child questions such as, 'What might happen next?', 'Why did that happen?' or 'Why did he say that?' If the child has even a limited reading range, simple books with tapes can be very helpful as the child can read the words while hearing them spoken.

Social Skills

Many children with dyslexia develop more slowly than children who do not have the condition. They also appear to have more difficulty acquiring information about everyday things that other children pick up quite naturally. Difficulties with time awareness may lead to confusion about dates of birthdays or whether Christmas comes before Easter. They may get the names of everyday objects mixed up or confuse relationships. One child, for example, thought he had three grandmothers. Adults may not even notice such little discrepancies but children are very quick to pick up on any perceived lapses by their peers. A simple mistake on the child's part may lead to teasing or worse. Therefore parents of children with dyslexia may need to devote some thought to how they can ensure that their child has appropriate social skills and does not lose face before other children. Parents who observe how a child interacts with peers may be able to intervene quietly and diplomatically in cases where the child may be at a disadvantage.

It is unfortunately true that a five or six year old who is not reading at the same level as classmates may already be seen by them as different and may be a target for bullying or exclusion. This danger may be lessened by a very pro-active parent who ensures that the child's self-esteem is maintained and who takes care that siblings or classmates are not allowed to tease or mock the child's reading difficulties. Talking to the child about the reading difficulty, putting it in context and not letting it dominate the child's life are very important.

Children who show indications of reading difficulty should be encouraged to develop any skills or talents that they show in other areas, such as drawing, dancing, swimming or drama. A child who is good at sport, for example, will often achieve sufficient success in that area to counterbalance any loss of esteem due to a reading difficulty.

Teachers will deal with the formal teaching process. It is important for parents, child minders or grandparents to remember that their teaching is informal. Sometimes the most important things are learned that way. Doing the shopping, baking scones, chatting, playing word games while sitting in traffic or commenting on television programmes can be entertaining and educational at the same time. Helping the child with dyslexia to acquire the skills needed to cope with school-based learning does not have to be a grim and boring task. Parents sometimes feel that unless they have a pencil and a workbook in hand they are not helping the child to learn. Nothing could be further from the truth. The grandmother who has time to tell stories, the grandfather who plays draughts, the parents who talk and listen to their child are all likely to contribute more to that child's development than the parent who insists on completing three pages of reading whatever the cost.

Discovering that a child has, or may have, a dyslexic-type problem can be very upsetting for a parent. There may be a temptation to focus in on the difficulty, to the exclusion of other aspects of the child's life, but it is important not to let that happen. The overall development of a healthy and happy child is the main priority. The fact that a child is not reading as well as little Jimmy who lives next-door is not important. What matters is that the child gets all the help possible and is not made to feel that parental love and approval are conditional on good school performance.

6. The Child at Home: Family Matters

This chapter will be of most use to parents. In it you will read about:

- Preparing the child for assessment;
- Dyslexia and family life;
- Supporting the younger child in the home;
- Supporting the older child in the home;
- Helping with homework – the primary school age;
- Supporting the child through the school system;
- Mediating with the outside world.

Preparing the Child for Assessment

If parents, in consultation with teachers, believe there are grounds for concern that a child has dyslexia, the next stage is a psycho-educational assessment. Having such an assessment should be a pleasant event in the child's life. Some commonsense points to bear in mind are listed below:

- Find out as much as you can about the assessment procedure in advance. The more prepared you are, the more relaxed you will be and this will be beneficial for the child.
- Be as honest and frank as you can. Note down points you consider relevant beforehand so that you do not forget them on the day. Note down any questions you would like to ask.
- Tell the child why you are visiting the psychologist. The reason is often because the child is having some difficulty in reading, writing or spelling.
- Present it in the most positive way you can – as something you have arranged to do so that you can help the child. Explain that the assessment will be of help to teachers in school in under-standing how the child learns.
- Explain what the psychologist will do. The child will be asked questions about school experiences and will be asked to do tasks like making designs with blocks, finding missing parts of a puzzle and some reading or spelling.
- Explain that it is not an exam. The child cannot fail. The psychol-ogist is only interested in finding out how the child thinks and learns.
- Tell your child where you are going, at what time and how long it will take.
- Try to ensure the child is well rested.
- Bring a nutritious snack and, if possible, build in a little treat afterwards.

After the assessment, the psychologist will probably give you some brief feedback. Using your own good judgement, tell the child as simply as possible what the psychologist has said, always stress-ing the most positive things. If you are upset or anxious about what you have been told, wait until you are feeling more positive before saying very much.

Dyslexia and Family Life

Nothing is nearer to parents' hearts than the welfare of their children. An illness or disability in one child affects the entire family. This is equally true of dyslexia. While dyslexia may not seem to be a big issue to people unaffected by it, it can have major implications for all the members of a family when a child is diagnosed with dyslexia.

It can be quite shocking for parents when they first get the diagnosis of dyslexia. They may feel angry with the school for not diagnosing the difficulty earlier. They may blame each other for things they did or did not do. They may worry that the child will never learn to read or write. They may feel embarrassed or ashamed of the difficulty. They may feel sad and fear for their child's future. They may over-react to the situation, thereby putting pressure on the child, and get the difficulty out of proportion. Whatever the immediate reaction, parents should allow themselves some time to come to terms with the fact that their child has a learning problem and to acquire as much information as possible about the condition and what they can do to help. The way in which the child reacts to the difficulty will be largely determined by the way in which parents approach the problem. If parents take a matter-of-fact approach, accepting that the child needs practical educational help and all the love and support they can provide, then the outcome is likely to be favourable. Children can, and do, cope with dyslexia. They grow up to be happy, useful and productive adults and the most important role in producing this outcome is played by parents.

Fathers sometimes have more difficulty in accepting the diagnosis than mothers. Dealing with schooling and homework often falls to the mother in the family. Fathers may not be quite as involved, particularly when the child is young. High-achieving fathers may have high expectations for their own children and be unwilling to admit difficulties. Fathers who have succeeded in life despite their own learning difficulties may think that too much fuss is being made of a dyslexic condition. However, it is very important that both parents are committed to whatever strategy is adopted to support the child at home and in school.

The child with dyslexia has special educational and emotional needs. Meeting these needs may involve spending extra time and money on the child. If both parents are in full agreement about the necessity for this, then it may be difficult but it can be done. If parents disagree about the management of their child's learning problem, this can cause conflict. Many parents report tensions arising from differing views on how much time is spent on homework, how much support is given, what effort is required from the child and how relations with the school and class teacher are to be managed. If money is scarce, the added expense of extra classes can add to the strain. Other children in the family may resent the fact that money is spent on tuition for the child with dyslexia but is not available to them for their hobbies or sports. These difficulties can be minimised if the family, as a whole, agree that the child with dyslexia needs extra support. Energy should, therefore, be put into providing this support and not diverted into issues of blame or allegations of favouritism.

Supporting the Younger Child in the Home

The first task that parents face is that of explaining dyslexia to the child. In order to do so, parents need to inform themselves. They then need to translate that information into simple language that the child can understand. Many children are very relieved to be given a diagnosis of dyslexia. They are often aware that a difficulty exists and may worry that they are stupid or even ill. The following are some hints that may be helpful when talking to your child:

- If your child is diagnosed as having dyslexia, then tell your child this. There is no reason to hide it.
- Explain that dyslexia is a very common condition and several other people in the school and maybe one or two in the class or in the family also have it.
- You can tell the child that dyslexia is just a big word to explain why some people find it hard to learn to read, write and spell. Everyone is different. We all have different strengths and weaknesses. Identify something the child does very well, whether it is sport, music, art or cooking. It could be that the child is good with animals, generous, popular, funny, loving – whatever. Find some real strength that the child has. This is most important. Then say that the child does not find reading and spelling as easy as these other things but that is how life is.
- Explain that this is not the fault of the child, the parent or the school. It is something that happens – like having fair hair, freckles or brown eyes.
- Let the child know that this explains why school learning is difficult.

- You can explain that it will be necessary to work very hard, maybe harder than others in the class to succeed but that it can be done, with proper help and support.
- Be prepared to discuss the problem with your child more than once. Do not assume that they will take it all in the first time. You may need to return to the subject over the coming years.
- If you have been angry with or critical of your child in the past because of homework/school difficulties then this is the time to apologise. Do not be afraid to say that you were wrong. Children can be very forgiving.
- If extra help is needed, either with a learning support teacher or outside of school, present this in the most positive light – as help rather than punishment.
- If extra help clashes with an activity that brings the child success, think very carefully before disturbing this arrangement.
- Make sure the child knows that while schoolwork is very important it is just one aspect of life.
- Ensure that the child knows that your love is not dependent on good results in schoolwork, that you value all of your children for their own sakes.
- If you are telling relatives or friends about the diagnosis of dyslexia in the child's hearing, be careful to be as positive as possible and not to tell them a different story than you told the child. Children very quickly pick up on discrepancies between what they have been told and what you really think.

It is also important that other children in the family understand about dyslexia. Sometimes a child may not want friends or siblings to know about the difficulty. This wish must be respected but it must be balanced by the fact that brothers and sisters need to know, so their support can be enlisted. It can be very demoralising for a ten-year-old who is struggling with homework to have a much younger child provide the answers or comment on the older child's mistakes.

If the dyslexia is acknowledged openly and siblings know that they all learn differently, then this is less likely to be a problem. Equally, other children in the family may feel neglected if too much parental energy goes into supporting the child with dyslexia. Children have a natural sense of fair play. If they see that a sibling is getting attention because of need and are reassured that, if they needed the extra care they would also receive it, they are usually understanding.

Supporting the Older Child in the Home

Increasingly, children are being diagnosed with dyslexia in early primary school. This is a very good development because younger children accept such events without too much questioning. However, it still happens that some students are not identified with dyslexia until entering secondary school or even later. This is most unfortunate because it means they may have already experienced failure and may have lost a great deal of confidence and self-esteem by then. Secondary difficulties such as school refusal, behavioural or emotional problems or withdrawal may have emerged. While most children are relieved to discover that there is a reason for the difficulties they experience, some react badly to being told that they have dyslexia. They may have no understanding of the condition. They may even fear that it is a psychiatric illness. They may deny it and refuse support, saying that there is no point. They may become angry with parents or school for not having identified the problem earlier or they may even want to opt out of school altogether. This reaction is understandable. Adolescence is a time when it is very important to be part of the group and any trait that makes one different is to be avoided. Any sign of weakness is to be hidden and self-consciousness and embarrassment can be agonising.

Teenagers who have had bad school experiences as a result of their dyslexia may need some formal or informal counselling before they begin to receive tuition. In order to benefit from remedial help, they must be mentally and emotionally ready. Students need to regain confidence in their own ability and believe that they can succeed.

The guidance counsellor at school may be able to help in this situation or parents may seek the advice of the assessing psychologist for referral to an outside counsellor. The family doctor should also be in a position to give advice on referral.

Parents can help by explaining dyslexia to the student, emphasising that it is not a defect but a learning difference and that it does not preclude school success. Second-level students should be able to read through their own psycho-educational assessment reports and begin to understand their own learning style. Adolescents, no less than their younger brothers and sisters, need to be reassured that parental love is not dependent on school success and all achievements are to be celebrated. At the same time, a fine line has to be walked between appreciating students' difficulties with academic work and allowing them to use dyslexia as an excuse for not trying.

Keeping a young teenager with dyslexia motivated to stay in school, to attend regularly and to work hard at schoolwork can be a challenge. Students, particularly those who did not receive early help, can become disillusioned with school and pessimistic about their own chances of examination success. They may miss a great deal of school time or want to drop out completely. Parents report that getting through second and third years is probably the most difficult in this regard. Many parents achieve this by taking a short-term approach. To an unhappy fourteen-year-old student, the idea of spending another four years in the school system may be unbearable, but staying on until Christmas may not seem so bad. By breaking up the school year into segments, say September to mid-term or mid-term to Christmas, and using a system of goals and rewards for each section, a year or two could be completed without too much trauma. The aim is to keep the student within the school system because dropping out before Junior Certificate really limits a person's career choices. It must also be borne in mind that the legal school-leaving age is sixteen.

Students who see themselves as failing in school desperately need to experience success in other aspects of life. Students with dyslexia may excel at science or maths, art or computer studies. On the other hand there may be no school subject for which they show a special aptitude. In such cases it is very important to maintain self-esteem by encouraging any out-of-school interests that bring satisfaction.

Students who experience no success at school may well be disruptive in class or engage in unacceptable behaviour. They may be suspended from school or at the least be regularly in trouble. Parents may have to exercise great imagination and ingenuity to find areas where their young teenagers can shine. Involvement in sports activities is an obvious area but many young people with dyslexia have poor motor co-ordination. Chess, debating, drama, scouting, youth clubs, involvement in community and voluntary groups such as Junior Red Cross or Young Citizens Parliament could all prove valuable. The most important thing is to identify an area where the student can gain feelings of competence and self-worth. Of course, at all times, the love and belief of their families will be of paramount importance. Home is where each student should feel safe and unthreatened, where there is no need to prove oneself to gain acceptance. More detailed information for supporting the student through second-level education is provided in Chapters 8, 9 and 10.

Helping with Homework: Primary School Age

Helping a child with dyslexia with homework can be a challenge, even for the best-organised parent. Sessions can end in tears and tantrums or with a smile and a sense of achievement. These two outcomes may be experienced on successive nights. Volumes have been written on the topic but in the end parents will work out the best system for themselves and for their child. Perhaps the most important thing to remember is that you are the parent, not the teacher (even if you have a doctorate in dyslexia), and that nothing is achieved when you and your child are tired, frustrated or upset. The common themes in the advice are listed below:

- Children with dyslexia often find it difficult to copy material from the blackboard, so the very first problem with homework may be that your child is not sure just what homework has been set. Questions to be answered may not have been fully copied, maths questions may not have been noted accurately and instructions given may have been forgotten.
- To cope with this problem it may be possible to enlist the help of the class teacher who would kindly agree to check the child's homework notebook after work has been assigned. You might arrange with the parent of a classmate that you can phone to get any missing information. Choose wisely, of course. Be sure to pick the parent of a child who takes accurate notes of homework. It is also worth checking with other parents whether information about trips, free days or special activities has been given out. Children with dyslexia are notorious for not remembering to pass on oral messages and even for losing printed ones. This is not deliberate. It is part of the difficulty.
- Having ensured that the correct homework has been identified, the child then needs to be settled comfortably at a table or desk, in good light and with the minimum of distraction. Some children may manage to complete homework while watching The Simpsons or feeding the cat but children with dyslexia generally cannot. They often have difficulty concentrating and once disrupted it may take some considerable time to get back on track. A supply of pens, pencils, erasers, rulers, notebooks, copies and

number squares needs to be available, as these items tend to go missing. In extreme cases a second set of schoolbooks might be secured, particularly if some books are kept in a school locker. That way there is always a set of books to hand. For the slightly older child, biros that can be erased such as the Papermate Replay are very handy. Child-friendly dictionaries with large print are also invaluable.

- The role of the parent ideally is to support by getting the child organised and then staying nearby to keep an eye on progress. It is not a good idea to sit at the child's elbow and oversee every word written. It is best to be available, if required, but not to assume responsibility for completion of the homework. That is the child's job. The older child may manage to complete home-work in privacy but the younger child almost invariably needs some support.

- If a child asks for help to read or explain a word or to spell a word, it is wise to do just what the child asks. It may be tempting to enter into a reading or spelling lesson, urging the child to sound out the word or to recall it from a previous task, but resist the urge. If a child finds that every time they ask a question the parent goes into teacher mode, then they may stop asking questions.

- It is quite common for children with dyslexia to have days when learning comes easily and days when they seem to have forgot-ten everything they ever knew. It is very frustrating for a parent who has carefully explained something on Monday night to find that on Tuesday night it is as if the child has never heard of the concept. Do not despair and do not be angry. Eventually the learning will take place.

- On the subject of teaching, this is the job of the teacher. Home-work is intended as a review or exercise on work done in the classroom. If the child does not understand, the parent may explain but should try to avoid teaching. The role of the parent is much too important in the child's life to confuse it with that of the teacher. A child has many teachers in the course of school life but only one Mum and Dad.

- If the child has a major problem with an item of homework, per-haps a note to the teacher in the homework journal is the best option. The teacher then knows that the child has not grasped the concept and may be able to repeat the lesson.

- Homework should not take up a child's entire leisure time. The class teacher can tell you how long homework should take.

Children in primary school are not usually expected to spend more than an hour or so at homework. If your child is spending much longer on tasks than normal, then it should be possible to arrange with the teacher that the child will spend an agreed amount of time on homework. If the child is exhausted and the parent is frustrated and needs to clear the kitchen table for dinner, then not much learning will take place, so it's best to call it a day.

- It is worth remembering that children with dyslexia do get very tired. Schoolwork is often a struggle and takes more effort than is required from other children. They may also attend extra classes outside of school or may have homework from their special needs teacher. In general, they do have to work harder at learning than other children, so at times they must be given a little leeway. However, parents also need to be on guard that the child does not use dyslexia as an excuse for not trying. It is a very difficult line for a parent to walk and it is just not possible to get it right all the time.

- Parents can only do as much as their circumstances will allow. Most people these days have very demanding work lives and in many families both partners work full-time. There has to be time to enjoy your child and to have fun. A child with dyslexia may be extremely capable in many ways and it is important to acknowledge that fact. They may also have unique talents and ways of viewing the world. Enjoy that difference and remember that, like all others, children with dyslexia grow up very fast.

Learning to enjoy reading

The early school years are spent learning to read. The remaining years are spent reading to learn. Fortunate people learn to read for pleasure. Children with dyslexia run the risk of thinking of reading purely in terms of schoolwork and do not easily associate it with fun.

Parents can really help in this area. Reading to young children is a wonderful way of opening their minds to the wider world, increasing their vocabulary and their understanding of language. Even when children with dyslexia learn to read reasonably well, they still benefit from having an adult read to them. They hear a fluent reader who pronounces words properly, who pauses at the appropriate places and who can explain the meaning of words or discuss the events in the story. This allows the child to appreciate the content of the story.

When a book or series is very popular, such as the Harry Potter stories, it is very important that the child with dyslexia keeps up with the trend. Parents can ensure that their child is up-to-date on the latest book by reading it with or for them. This will not make the child lazy or reluctant to read alone. On the contrary it will encourage a love of reading. Books on tape are a great way of passing a long car journey. Disputes about space, cries of, 'Are we there yet?' and even travel sickness can be eliminated by listening to the children's choice of books during the long holiday drive.

Paired reading

Paired reading is an ideal technique for parents to use when reading for pleasure with the child and it is also very successful in improving reading ability. It has been recommended by learning support teachers for years and schools will usually have information leaflets and videos on how to do it. The thinking behind this technique is that daily practice of the art of reading, without any formal teaching strategy being used, helps the child to read while enjoying the process. The reading takes place at a different time and in a different atmosphere to homework. Curled up on a sofa in front of the fire would be ideal.

The child chooses a book. Parental guidance may be needed to ensure that the book chosen is not way out of the child's reading level but the important thing is that the child wants to read that book. Then parents set aside a particular slot of five to seven minutes every day, during which they read together with the child. The parent adjusts reading speed to match that of the child. They say the words together. If the child finds a word difficult the parent reads it. The child repeats the word. They move on and the flow of reading is not interrupted by any attempt to make the child sound out the word. If the child would like to read alone, an agreed signal (say, a tap on the book) can be given and the parent stays silent until the end of the session. This technique is beautifully simple, yet it is very effective. To get the most benefit from paired reading, it is important that it is done every evening over a period of weeks.

Of course, paired reading could also be done by grandparents or other adults with whom the child is comfortable. The idea is for a pleasant, entertaining and enjoyable reading session to take place.

Helping the child to learn spellings

There are many suggestions about how best to teach spellings but they are all based on the same fundamental principles. It is widely agreed that children with dyslexia benefit from a multi-sensory teaching approach. This means that a combination of senses should be used – hearing, seeing and touching. The history books report that in the old monastic schools children were taught the alphabet by making the letters in dough, baking them and then eating them. What a lovely way to learn and what a lot those early teachers knew about acquiring knowledge.

Today a parent with the time and energy could use some cookie dough to help a child to 'internalise' a difficult word. A simpler and less fattening technique is the following, often called the Look-Say-Cover-Write-Check method. Best results are obtained if no more than five words are learned at a time. The words can be written, formed with plastic or wooden letters, traced on sandpaper, rough carpet or on a sand tray. The child looks at the word until it is known. The word is spoken and explained if necessary. It could be put in a sentence. Then the word is covered and the child writes the word and says it. Next the child checks the written version of the word against the original. If the spelling is correct then the next word can be tackled. If the spelling is not correct then a little more time has to be spent on looking at and repeating the word.

Supporting the Child through the School System

Recent developments encourage much more participation by parents of children with special educational needs in the management of their children's education. The role of parents is recognised by the Department of Education and Science in its legislation and in its recommendations. The Education Act of l998 requires schools to produce a policy for pupils with disabilities, outlining how they cater for such students and setting up a grievance procedure that parents can use if they feel that adequate support is not provided. The Education for Persons with Special Educational Needs Act 2004 states its purpose is:

> To provide that people with special educational needs shall have the same right to avail of, and benefit from, appropriate education as do their peers who do not have such needs ... [and] ... to provide for

the greater involvement of parents of children with special educational needs in the education of their children.

The *Learning Support Guidelines* issued in 2000 state:

> If, following diagnostic assessment, it is agreed that the pupil should receive supplementary teaching, the parents can contribute to the development and implementation of their child's individual profile and learning programme (IPLP) by discussing the learning targets for their child and by identifying activities that can be implemented at home to support the work of the school in achieving the agreed targets.

The underlying thinking is clear. Parents should be involved in discussing the supplementary teaching their children receive at school and how this can be best supported at home. Parents are to be involved in all aspects of their children's education and most schools welcome the input from interested and supportive parents.

When a child has a specific learning disability, supporting the child through the school system depends less on legislation, perhaps, than on developing a good working relationship with the school and keeping informed on how educational policy impacts on the child with dyslexia.

Developing and maintaining a mutually trusting and understanding relationship between schools and teachers requires time and effort on both sides. Parents can best help to foster this by being honest, open and realistic about their child's needs and abilities. Information such as results of psycho-educational assessment, the amount of time spent on homework and the help that is given by parents or outside tutors is important to teachers. It helps them to evaluate the child's learning strengths and weaknesses and in preparing education plans for the child in school.

Keeping the school informed of your child's educational needs can be more difficult at secondary than at primary level. A copy of any psycho-educational assessment report should be supplied to the school principal but this will not necessarily make its way to all subject teachers. A brief summary of the report, with any relevant recommendations, could be sent in to all the child's teachers in September and also given to teachers at parent/teacher meetings. It may be necessary to make several copies and give one to every subject teacher every year.

It is important to be realistic about your child. A child, who has been assessed as of high academic ability but is achieving at an average or lower level is likely to be frustrated and even angry. This child may not be easy to handle in a classroom situation. A child who does not have great academic ability must be allowed to work at a pace suited to that ability and parents must recognise that fact and not expect unreasonably high achievement. It is important to realise that every difficulty a child experiences in the classroom is not necessarily caused by dyslexia. There are other factors involved, such as the personality of the child, the overall ability, the attitude to work and to authority. Children with dyslexia can be forgetful, disorganised and even disruptive in class. They are normal children and vary enormously in both the degree of their dyslexia and in their other traits.

It is also important, of course, to act as an advocate for your child by explaining both needs and abilities. Parents may be told that each child in a class or a school has to be treated the same way in the interests of fair play. This is not necessarily the best approach. Treating children according to their own individual needs is much fairer. If one child feels ill and is sent home, the other children are not sent home too – this is not unfair. If children with dyslexia need some adjustments to the amount or type of homework that they do, this is not unfair. What would be unfair would be to make the ill child remain at school or to expect the child with dyslexia to spend three times as long on homework as the other children.

Children with dyslexia often have great competence and ability in a variety of areas. It is not boastful to make sure that teachers and other relevant people are made aware of this. At primary level the class teacher will know your child well and be aware that while spelling may be a problem, Maths is a strength. At second level this does not apply. Second-level teachers may see three hundred students in a week and cannot be expected to know the full profile of each.

The other way in which you can support your child is by learning as much as possible about dyslexia and by keeping up to date on developments within the education system to support students. It is not wise to rely solely on the school to carry out this function; as a parent you should make this your business. There is a great deal of information out there and it pays to be aware. Books such as the one you are currently reading and *Lost for Words* by Wyn McCormack give you the basic information. Updated information is contained on the following websites:

- Department of Education and Science www.education.ie;
- The Special Education Support Service www.sess.ie;

- The Dyslexia Association of Ireland www.dyslexia.ie;
- The Association for Higher Education Access and Disability www.ahead.ie.

The latest information on topics such as exemption from the study of Irish, reasonable accommodations in state examinations, assistive technology, up-coming conferences/parents courses and support services at third level can be obtained from these websites. This information is directly relevant to the child with dyslexia and their parents. At the very least it may help to ease the student's progress through the system. At best it may make the difference between attaining entry to a desired course/career and settling for a second choice.

Mediating with the Outside World

If you think back to the time before your child demonstrated a learning difficulty, can you honestly say that you were aware of dyslexia? In all probability you had heard the word or some basic facts but never stopped to think what it might involve for a person who had that condition.

Other people are no different. Over the years your child will come across many people who do not know much about dyslexia or who may even have totally mistaken ideas about its effects. You may have to explain to grandparents, extended family, friends and perhaps even teachers that your child is a normal, healthy and capable child who just happens to have dyslexia.

Dyslexia can, as the cliché goes, 'cause smart people to act dumb'. To the uninitiated it may look as if your child is being careless, stupid, stubborn or downright uncooperative. Children with dyslexia may have great trouble in remembering quite simple things and in organising themselves. They may do the wrong homework, lose their belongings, forget to deliver messages, get details or instructions mixed up and be perpetually late for appointments. It is all too easy to say, 'He may have a reading difficulty but why doesn't he do what he's told?' As a parent you may have to explain to a football coach, a scout leader or the parent of a classmate that dyslexia affects much more than reading ability. Poor short-term memory, short attention span, motor co-ordination difficulties, poor sense of time and a tendency to get names and dates mixed up are all part of dyslexia. If you can explain this to a person who is feeling frustrated by your child's behaviour, then they may look at the child in quite a different light and be prepared to see the child's ability as well as the disability.

Caring for the carers

This is a very important topic. Parents invest time, money and a great deal of energy in rearing their children. This is even truer of parents of children with dyslexia. Caring and supporting is a demanding business but it does not have to occupy all your time and energy. You are entitled to leisure and some time for your own interests.

It can be difficult to keep the learning needs of your child in perspective but, realistically, there is a limit to what parents can be expected to do. In many households both partners work long hours and have other family duties and commitments. There will be times when you do not have the time, energy or patience to respond to your child's needs as you feel you should. There will be times when parents are quite frustrated and disappointed at the lack of a child's progress or at how quickly information is forgotten. There will be worries when tests and examination results are disappointing, despite the best efforts of everyone concerned. Parent/teacher meetings can be quite stressful. There may be differences of opinion between parents, between parents and child or between parents and school about how the dyslexic problem is to be managed. All of this takes its toll on parents and on family members. Sometimes it is necessary to step back a little and distance yourself from the situation. If parents concentrate too much of their energy on dealing with a learning difficulty, it can interfere with their own normal lives, with sports, hobbies or social interaction. All of these are necessary to a balanced life and it is the right of every person to take some time for themselves. If you do not look after your own well-being, you will not be able to look after your children. You are often told not to be too demanding of your children – you should not be too demanding of yourself either.

7. The Primary School Child: Child Development

This chapter will be of most use to parents. In it you will read about:

- Stages of child development – early primary school years;
- Stages of child development – later primary school years;
- Emotional needs.

Before looking at the features that are unique to the child with dyslexia it is perhaps worth looking at developmental stages through which children are passing during their primary school years. They are becoming more developed and sophisticated in the way they think, learn and monitor their own learning, how they recognise, name and manage emotion and how they relate to others. There are important milestones to be reached and hurdles to be negotiated.

Once again we can refer to research studies over the years that have given us insight into stages of development through which the child passes.

Stages of Child Development: Early Primary School Years

At this time young children are beginning to recognise their strengths and understand that they are individuals with abilities. They need to experience a sense of industry and accomplishment through being able to complete tasks successfully. On the emotional level they are eager to please and thus they need frequent recognition and praise. On the cognitive level children at this age are becoming more capable of thinking, though still in a concrete manner rather than abstractly. They can think about situations and solve problems within their own experience. At this time their attitude to school and what it has to offer them is being established. Their roles within the group are being formed.

During these years the child is being introduced to reading and writing skills. A survey of the aims and objectives as outlined in the primary school English language curriculum indicates how far reaching and ambitious these are. In the junior and senior infant classes they are expected to develop 'concepts of language and print' and 'competence, confidence and the ability to write independently'. This includes activities such as listening to stories, learning nursery rhymes, playing language games with sounds, action songs and poems, writing and reading their writing aloud.

By the end of second class children are expected to 'pursue individual interests through independent reading of fiction and non-fiction' and are expected to discuss what they have read. They have been taught the basic strategies for comprehension. They are learning how to write in 'a variety of genres' and how to make notes while they read.

By third class they are using the library freely, looking at tables of contents, using a dictionary and finding the pronunciation of words. They are writing regularly over a period of time. They are expected to present work with a clear sequence of ideas and to have begun to self-correct their work.

Children without a disability respond eagerly to every initiative because most children at this stage are eager to learn. Children with dyslexia, like their peers, are eager to learn but these are the very activities that present them with difficulties. Letter–sound matching, phonological analysis (sounding out words, recognising same/different sounds of letters and clusters of letters), handwriting, spelling, sequencing and order may all be problematic. They are experiencing varying degrees of success depending on their form of dyslexia. At first they do not understand why they are falling behind. Later they may adopt unhelpful attitudes to *protect* themselves from further failure. The more advanced the learning task, the more noticeable the difference between themselves and their peers. The danger is that the initial enthusiasm for learning begins to wane.

The support available for children is crucial. It is important at this stage to build up their sense of accomplishment through activities and skills that are not affected by dyslexia. Reading and writing are but two skills in a wide range of skills where children can be competent. The importance of literacy skills needs to be kept in proportion relative to the whole child's development. They need to know such skills are important and they will eventually learn them, although at a slower rate than their peers. Parents and teachers can help them to develop strategies for learning by getting to know how they solve problems in activities other than reading and writing. This will demand from parents an investment of effort and time and from the teacher creative activities and teaching methods appropriate to their learning style.

Under the staged plan of learning support in school dyslexia will, in all likelihood, not be formally diagnosed until children are nearer to seven-and-a-half years old. This is for two reasons. The delay may be developmental, health-related or circumstantial and not as a result of dyslexia. It can be difficult to be certain of the cause of delay and difficulty prior to that. Secondly, the school will operate on the principle of early intervention before formal assessment. Once children have been recognised as having a difficulty or a delay in learning to read and write, the school should put in place additional learning support for a fixed period and should review the progress at the end of the period. Then, depending on the results, the decision will be made to continue the learning support, to withdraw the support if they have 'caught up' or to refer children on to an educational psychologist for full psycho-educational assessment.

All this needs to be dealt with very positively. As a parent you may begin to feel anxious for the child and unsure about how to proceed. Reading for pleasure with the child, playing visual games such as *I Spy* or *Spot the Difference*, tracing, copying activities, model building and word games are all ways to help to develop pre-reading skills. Many children with dyslexia do not pick up new words as easily as children who do not have dyslexia. Speaking clearly, repeating new words, explaining what they mean, engaging them in conversation, asking their opinion are all very ordinary but very essential ways of developing language. Other siblings may try to intervene when they see the child having difficulty finding the right word but it is better to accustom them to wait for a reply. Insisting, tactfully, on full sentences and helping with word-finding will assist in developing an awareness of the structure of language.

It is also important to keep in close touch with teachers and consolidate at home some of the lessons being taught in school. There are a number of early learning programmes that can be used at home, with no teaching background required, such as PAT (phonological awareness training), Toe-by-Toe (available from Surgisales) or ETC Consult (Appendix B). There are also many learning games that can be used as a family activity.

Children are alert and register the attitudes of people who are significant in their lives towards their difficulty. At this stage they usually respect rules and look up to authority figures. This is a time when correction of failure needs to be minimised. At home and at school the emphasis needs to be on what they can do, not on what they cannot accomplish. Homework needs to be tailored and the time it takes limited to what is reasonable and within their attention span. As they get older, rules can be made into contracts or mutual agreements.

Children at this stage are also beginning to be very sensitive to their place in the group and are adopting roles in relation to the group. With confidence, they will be active participants. Where there is a poor sense of competence and a perception of failure, they may well adopt attitudes of learned helplessness or withdraw from the group. Where children have begun to have a stable sense of self, which is evident when they can describe themselves as having certain characteristics, likes, dislikes and feelings, they are less likely to feel threatened in the group. This raising of self-awareness is closely related to how they value themselves that, in turn, has been learned from how they think others value them. If they are to develop a good self-image and self-esteem, children need to be regarded as individuals without reference to the achievement of their peers.

At home parents can minimise situations where children may fail by making sure that tasks are structured and within their capabilities and that the children are rewarded for their effort. Similar criteria are relevant in school. The classic spelling test needs to be individualised for children with dyslexia so that there is a minimum number of spellings they are sure to remember and that their progress is marked by reference to their own previous spelling achievement and not with reference to others' achievement. If a child can accurately recall three spellings this week, try four the next week. Gradually increase the load when the child is ready to move on. Teach strategies such as visually remembering parts of words or even whole words, making associations between words and objects or grouping related pieces of information.

By the time children are ten, they have acquired most of the tools needed to be an efficient learner. Their preferred way of carrying out an intellectual task should be evident at this time. Are they impulsive or reflective? Do they look at the whole picture first or focus on the detail? Do they like to study alone away from everyone or in the middle of the action? Do they prefer to have the heat at full blast or sit with the window wide open in the middle of January? Do they draw diagrams to revise or prefer to listen to you reading the chapter? These may seem irrelevant but in fact they are the indicators of what is termed *learning style*. Everyone has a personal, preferred way of doing things and one achieves best when the environment is conducive to learning.

This is not to say that ways of doing things cannot be taught. Often time and energy are wasted because one insists on personally reinventing the wheel. By recognising a child's learning style you are providing the tools to efficient learning. Thus if a child always draws pictures, teach them how to make mind-maps of the chapter of history to be learnt. Such mind-maps could use pictures instead of words. If they like to listen, put the chapter on tape and have them devise a story around the facts. If they love colour and shape, use colour coding for mathematical symbols and signs. If they cannot remember how to add and subtract 'in their head', then give them an abacus to count with. Apply such concrete materials to the other mathematical shapes until the child is ready to move on.

Stages of Child Development: Later Primary School Years

Having successfully negotiated the first five years of primary school and having begun to develop a sense of self as competent, children in the senior primary school are becoming more interested in aspects of identity such as appearance and gender role. They have developed an ability not only to generalise from individual experiences but also to generate hypotheses about how things might be. They can now think abstractly. They become more involved with the group and with co-operation. This means that rules are more meaningful when they are negotiated and agreed upon. Peer acceptance and the ability to take personal decisions are increasingly important. At this stage physical development can affect self-confidence and consequently behaviour. At the same time they are now better able to take another's point of view and understand it. Literacy and school achievement may have a lower place on the list of priorities.

For the parent, knowledge is power. The methods of dealing with the situation may need to change. Having a say, not losing out on group activities and being part of the group are all very important to the child at this stage. However, while some things can be negotiated, there remain basic non-negotiable ground rules. If this is understood for all activities then it will be easier to apply a similar method when encouraging habits of study and accepting additional support.

Children with dyslexia need greater support to become the confident, competent persons they have the potential to be. Characteristically, they may experience a delay in becoming automatic at reading and writing, and the gap between academic potential and achievement may get wider as the work becomes more demanding. While they know and have developed skills in other areas, they realise deep down that ultimately the ability to read and write is important for their future. By the time they face into secondary school, it is important to have developed an interest in knowledge and some awareness of how they work best, as well as good strategies that help them to store information.

In the senior primary school days learning skills can be reinforced in a variety of informal ways. Basic to all learning is the ability to hold information in attention long enough to process it. One does not learn what one did not notice. First, one pays attention; then one stores the information; later, to recall the information, one has to find the file in which it is stored. Children with dyslexia experience difficulty with holding attention and storing information in a systematic way. Apart from reading and writing they need to develop ways and means of focusing their attention and connecting information. Techniques can be used to develop attention by using strategies such as demanding eye contact or giving an instruction and asking for it to be repeated. Later they form the habit of recollecting or reminding themselves at the beginning of each study session of what they are about to do. Learning will not take place with a divided attention. All distracting stimuli should be eliminated, whether auditory, visual or postural. This is why it is important to understand how the child learns best. Not everybody can sit upright at a desk but nobody can learn efficiently with one eye on the moving frames on the television set!

Visual attention to detail can be developed by playing memory games when walking down the street. Questions can be asked such as, 'What colours were in the dress shop window?' or 'How many instruments were in the music shop window?' Develop habits of rehearsing heard information, associating it with a significant number, picture or detail such as recalling a person by the colour and shape of her handbag.

Children in the senior primary classes are expected to take part in discussions at school. The more they are included in family discussions, where their opinion is asked for and valued, the more confidently they will present themselves in class. When they can discuss in a *safe* environment, where everybody is expected to make a contribution and where everybody's opinion is valued, the child will learn how to take turns, to listen, to respect and probably to revise. When they are not listened to, they are more likely to be loud and uncompromising in their statements.

Emotional Needs

So far we have dealt with stages of development and processes for learning. But what happens when the stages are not being traversed as smoothly as the above would suggest? How does the parent deal with the *wobbles* of identity, the 'I'm stupid' period, the learned helplessness, the switching off and the bullying that may happen because the child is different?

As the work at school becomes more demanding, children with dyslexia are faced with a number of possible ways of responding. How they *feel* about the challenge can have a significant effect on how they behave. When self-esteem is low you will hear expressions of anger, boredom, anxiety, being fed-up and being useless. These may translate themselves into *actions* such as evading doing the work, excuses as to why it is not finished, giving up easily, being noisy and boisterous, statements such as 'I can't do that', hiding work, attention seeking, being easily led and so on.

At this point you need to get below the surface to find out what messages children are giving themselves or what patterns of *thinking* underpin their behaviour and feelings. People with low self-esteem tend to confirm their low opinion of themselves. They select what details of an incident they choose to remember, usually the ones that illustrate to them their *uselessness* and failure. They use absolute judgements such as, 'I'm no good at anything'. They make inaccurate associations, 'I can't read, therefore I'm stupid'. They take all criticism personally. Each of these perceptions needs to be explored.

Building up self-esteem is a slow and painstaking process and requires ongoing reinforcement. The trap is lowering expectations for children when what they need is to be challenged in such a way that they learn to succeed and use failure constructively and in perspective. They need to know that you believe they can and will succeed. This brings us back to learning to be industrious. This skill is learnt when the tasks they are given are in part within their competence and in part a challenge to go beyond their present stage. Children can be *walked through* the task by judicious prompting, explanation and demonstration, repeated as often as needed until such time as they know they can do it on their own. We have already noted that children with dyslexia take considerably longer to become automatic in a task. By giving them the opportunity to become expert by multiple repetitions you are also building up self-confidence and self-esteem.

Establishing habits of self-reflection is integral to this process. The child needs to become as independent and self-directive as possible. Creating a learning checklist/diary in which they keep track of their own learning behaviour is one way of encouraging good habits. A checklist of items that helped in study might include statements such as:

- Ignored noise around me;
- Turned off the IPOD and mobile phone;
- Cleared desk of clutter;
- Quietened myself before starting;
- Followed my homework plan.

Where the item cannot be ticked off as satisfactory on a particular occasion, this action is targeted for improvement at the next session. Thus actions are seen in context and failures are seen as possible to correct.

It is very difficult to separate the different layers at which one functions. As observed above, feeling informs thought and vice versa; thought and feeling inform behaviour. Children with dyslexia need to understand the nature of their disability if they are to integrate it into their picture of who they are. Poor acceptance of the disability can take the form of denial. Emergent teenagers, particularly, often prefer to ignore their differences at school rather than avail of the supports that could improve their difficulties.

At all stages the fact that children with dyslexia are different leaves them vulnerable both to being bullied and to perpetrating bullying behaviours. A common insult is to call children with dyslexia 'stupid' because they cannot get their spelling right, because they are clumsy and cannot keep up at football or because the class has to wait for them while they look for the right page. However, low self-esteem generated by a sense of being no good can result in aggressive, bullying behaviour. In each case the behaviour needs to be confronted and each party led to understand the impropriety of their behaviour. Parents and school need to work together at resolving the issues.

Children who are the victims of bullying behaviour will need to develop a stronger sense of self. How is this achieved? By focusing on accomplishments, by extending the range of activities and interests, by getting involved in group activities in which they are successful and by helping them to understand difference. A useful strategy is to create a Positives diary in which they record the happy and successful achievements of each day such as, 'Finished my homework', 'Didn't give up when I couldn't solve the maths problem' or 'Held my tongue when I wanted to shout out the answer'. Establishing a reward structure where the achievement is recognised not only by the adult but claimed by children themselves, is another method of helping them to know their own strengths.

Often children with dyslexia are afraid of telling others about their difficulty for fear of the perceptions others may have of what it means to be dyslexic. Giving them the opportunity to explain to others how it feels to be dyslexic can be an enlightening experience. It is a two-way transaction. Often they do not know that everybody does not experience the world as they do. How can others know how they feel if they do not listen to them? By giving them opportunities to explain to others, perhaps a class group, we are sending out the message, 'It is all right to think and feel like this'. In Frank (2002) the reader is invited to perform a number of everyday activities that mimic the difficulties experienced by people with dyslexia in order to get a deeper understanding. Similar exercises that are non-threatening could be used in class and with siblings to illustrate the point.

And what of the child who becomes the bully? There are many underlying reasons why children bully other children. Top of the list must be a sense of powerlessness and the need to dominate. Bullies become expert at finding the Achilles heel of their victims and often appeal to the support of their gang of followers. Sometimes they are unaware of the hurt they cause. Helping them to take another's point of view is important for their social development. Denial and poor self-esteem can express itself in aggressive and inappropriate behaviour. Consequently, the underlying low self-esteem may have to be addressed. The social effects of bullying need to be made very clear to the child and a clear system of reward and reprimand put in place to reverse the behavioural patterns that have become habitual.

In each case, it may be necessary to involve professional counsellors to help address the issues. Counsellors may work out a programme of behaviour therapy. There are a variety of approaches that can be used. Some therapists deal with the individual situations and facts of a particular incident. They intervene with suggested solutions rather than a lengthy analysis of incidents and causes. Others take a 'no blame' approach, which allows early intervention without attributing blame to one side or the other. Referral to the Anti-bullying Unit in Trinity College Dublin is always a possibility, if one lives within the catchment area. School counsellors, NEPS psychologists and psychologists within the Health Boards can be consulted.

However it is managed, bullying needs to be dealt with openly and in a concerted manner. School and home must work together with common, agreed policies and action. As with all abuse, secrecy is the lethal weapon of the abuser. Children who bully depend on others not speaking up and children who are bullied are often in fear of speaking up. Keeping the lines of communication open between parents and children may not save them from being bullied or from bullying others but these situations are less likely to occur if they know they can tell adults how they feel.

8. Coping at Second Level: Educational Choices

This chapter will be of most use to parents and students with dyslexia at second level. At the beginning of second level, students are still very young and parents have a key role in making educational decisions. As students mature, they should take an increasing responsibility for decisions so that by the time they are in senior cycle, they are deciding about their future with guidance from parents and teachers. In this chapter you will read about the following educational choices:

- Choice of school;
- Subject choice;
- Choices in the state examination system;
- Choices after Junior Certificate;
- Choices after Leaving Certificate.

Key educational decisions should be based on the child's abilities and interests and on the opportunities available. If students enjoy the subjects/courses they are studying, it increases motivation and helps them achieve. Education has become increasingly more flexible with new courses and new routes to qualifications. Students with dyslexia tend to have an ability profile with clearly defined strengths and weaknesses. The flexibility in the education system enables them to concentrate increasingly on their strengths as they progress through second level to third level and further education.

Choice of School

Deciding which second-level school is the most suitable for a student with dyslexia is a key decision for parents. Some parents may not have a choice since there may be only one school for the area. Other parents have a choice, particularly in city areas. To make the best choice, the parents need to have as much information as possible. There are many different factors to be considered when choosing a school. There is no perfect school that meets all criteria. Parents need to decide on what they consider to be the most important criteria that will best meet their child's needs.

Below are some points to consider when choosing a school.

Class placement

How does the school place students in classes? Most schools have more than one class in each year group. Different ways to place students in classes include:

- *Mixed ability*: Students are randomly placed in class groups so each class has students with varying abilities;
- *Setting*: Students are assessed in individual subjects, usually Irish, English and Maths. They are then placed in a class according to their ability in that subject. Thus a student may be in a top Maths class and a weaker English class;
- *Streaming*: Students are placed in classes by their performance at assessment. Thus there may be a top ability, middle ability and weakest ability class;
- *Banding*: This is an attempt to merge mixed ability and streaming. The year group may be divided into two halves, based on

ability, and then classes are formed on a mixed-ability basis inside each half.

What is the most appropriate class placement for an individual student with dyslexia who may have an uneven profile of ability? Mixed ability and setting both have advantages. Mixed ability allows the student to benefit from the range of ideas and stimuli in the class, while setting allows the student to specialise in subjects they are good at. Streaming is criticised for the effect it can have on morale and motivation in lower streams. Students may become disaffected with resulting discipline problems. For students with dyslexia this may be the worst scenario. They may be placed in a low stream because of weaker verbal skills but the class might not provide the challenge and stimulation to cater for their strengths.

Discipline

Students with dyslexia tend to be disorganised. They need a clearly organised classroom with clear instructions and a sense of order, as they may need to concentrate quite hard to interpret their teacher's instructions. Some students learn much more from listening attentively than they do from reading from a textbook. They require a well-structured and disciplined atmosphere in which to do this.

Size of school

Large schools (schools of over 500 pupils) can provide a wider range of subjects. With more choice, students are more likely to find subjects in which they can do well. Smaller schools have a reduced range of subjects, which may be a disadvantage. However, the smaller school provides an environment where each student is known by all the staff, which can have a beneficial effect on self-esteem and strengthen a feeling of being part of the school community. There may also be smaller classes and less streaming.

Class size

It is very much to the student's advantage if class sizes are small. In a small class the teacher has more time to pay individual attention to students. However, in most publicly funded schools classes are at the maximum class size. This is 30 students or 24 in classes where there is a practical element such as Science or Home Economics.

School attitude to learning difficulties

Some schools can be very supportive of the needs of students with diverse learning difficulties, including dyslexia, and have structures in place to assist them. In meeting with the principal of a school for the first time to discuss the needs of the student, it will become apparent whether the school has a supportive attitude or not.

Unfortunately, it has been the experience of some parents that not all schools are supportive. Some schools are oversubscribed with many more applicants than places. Parents have spoken about the fact that some principals attempt to persuade them that the school would not be suitable for their child with a learning difficulty. They point to a lack of resources and argue that other schools might have more. They may even mention the *academic* ethos of their own school or point to the fact that all students must study one or even two foreign languages. In some cases such persuasion occurs despite the fact that the student's siblings are already attending the school. It seems to be inequitable that a school is willing to enrol some children in a family but is unwilling to enrol the child with learning difficulties. Reluctance to enrol students with learning difficulties means that up to 10 per cent of the population may not be considered appropriate intake. Imagine if this was a physical disability and the schools could argue that a child with glasses or a limp could not be catered for adequately and that the appropriate placement was in other schools.

The reality is that under the Education Act all schools should provide equality of access and appropriate educational provision to meet the needs of the child. The school cannot discriminate on the grounds of disability. Also it is unfair on schools with inclusive policies if such schools are expected to enrol a disproportionate number of students with learning difficulties. With the media focusing on league tables based on student results, the true achievement of such schools may not be appreciated.

If parents have decided to send their child to a particular school and have concerns about the possible school attitude, one strategy is that they do not tell the school about the needs of the student until they have first been offered a place in the school. At this stage discussions should then be centred on how the school can best meet the needs of the student. If parents meet difficulties, they should use their increased rights under the Education Act and ask to see the school policy on enrolment, particularly with reference to students with learning difficulties. If the principal makes a comment such as that the school does not cater for students with a learning difficulty, ask that this be put into writing.

One very immediate way to improve provision for students with dyslexia and other learning difficulties is to provide in-service training for teachers. Many teachers at second level have received no training on the topic of dyslexia either in pre-service or in-service courses. Schools are allowed one day for in-service training for the whole staff during the academic year. Parents could, either themselves or through the Parents' Association, request that the school consider holding an in-service day on the topic of dyslexia. The Special Education Support Service (SESS) provides training for teachers on the topic of dyslexia when requested by the school principal. Such training is particularly relevant in view of recent legislation.

Learning support/resource teaching

Students, on entrance to second-level, may still need additional help. Such help may be provided by a learning support teacher or a resource teacher. Are such facilities available? Does the student meet the criteria to access them?

Friends

In some cases students with learning difficulties may have difficulty making new friends easily. This may be the result of past bullying or low self-esteem. Such students might have a small number of friends. It will help the transition to second level if they go to the same school as their friends.

Extra-curricular activities

Self-esteem can be fragile in students with dyslexia. They may have experienced difficulty and failure with the academic part of the curriculum. However, they can achieve success and peer recognition in other areas such as the extra-curricular activities organised by the school. Some schools put on a wide range of activities that can include sports, debating, drama, a school bank, camera clubs and social activities such as Amnesty International. Parents should check the range of activities available.

Subject Choice

Subject choice is of critical importance to students with dyslexia. The average student may have individual preferences about subjects but is likely to do, on average, equally well in different subjects. Students with dyslexia may find some subjects at second level in which they will do exceptionally well and others where they face failure from first year. At primary level the main challenge for students is the development of literacy and numeracy. This may mean that for a major portion of the school day, students with dyslexia may have been confronted by tasks that they found difficult and struggled to achieve in. Now at second level, while they must continue to develop literacy and numeracy, they may find subjects in which they can achieve well. If students can access the information in a subject and communicate such knowledge in an exam, they will achieve. This success helps with self-esteem and motivation.

There are no clear rules about subject choice, as each child with dyslexia has a unique profile of strengths and weaknesses. However, here are some pointers to help with choice:

- Languages may prove to be a difficulty for some. Indicators that a student may have difficulties with languages are poor achievement in English and Irish, poor aural and oral ability, poor phonic skills and poor memory of sounds. A student who has good oral and aural skills may succeed well in languages, particularly as a large part of the marks in the state exams are awarded to the oral and aural elements of the exam. It is a widely held belief that a student needs a foreign language for entry to third level. However, it is only in the National University of Ireland (NUI) colleges that this is an entry requirement and the student with dyslexia may apply for an exemption. Other third-level colleges do not require that students have a foreign language for entry to the college. However, a language is likely to be a course requirement on courses where students intend to study languages.

- Subjects that require answers containing factual information may be easier than subjects in which answers are in essay-type format where the student has to analyse and sequence information to structure the answer. Therefore, Science may be easier to achieve in than English or History.
- Some subjects such as Technical Graphics, Maths and Accounting rely on the student learning skills by doing several examples of the same task with different information. There is less of a reliance on memorising of facts. For the student with short-term memory difficulties, this may help.
- Some students with dyslexia have excellent spatial/visual relations and will do well in subjects such as Art, Construction Studies and Technical Graphics.
- Continuous assessment may help the student with short-term memory difficulties. Some subjects such as Art, Home Economics, Engineering, Construction Studies and Religion have a project or journal to be filled in prior to the terminal exam and marks are awarded for such work.

At senior cycle it is even more important that the subjects taken suit the student. Firstly, as in Junior Cycle, motivation and interest will be maintained if the student enjoys the subjects studied. Secondly, the Leaving Certificate is the gateway to higher and further education. This is a key moment in career choice for students. In Ireland, because students may take seven subjects or more for the Leaving Certificate, it is still possible to leave many paths open and not narrow one's options after the Junior Certificate. This is generally a good thing as it gives students time to mature before making critical career decisions. In the UK, this is the time when students specialise and take a narrow range of subjects for A levels.

However, in Ireland where such a wide range of subjects is offered, option structures may be restricted and students with dyslexia may be at a disadvantage. They may have to take subjects that are verbally based and they may not be able to specialise in their best subjects. As an example, take a student with dyslexia who is very proficient in the Maths, Business and technical subjects. This student may have to take English, Irish and a third language as three of their seven subjects. Unless the option structure is very open, it is possible they may have to take other verbally based subjects such as Economics or History. If the same student could choose subjects such as English, Maths, Physics, Chemistry, Accounting, Technical Graphics and Engineering, it would certainly improve their chances of maximising points for the CAO system as well as giving them subjects they may enjoy studying. In Chapter 4, the example is given of a student in 2004 who, by being able to take the subjects of Technical Graphics and Applied Maths outside school hours, increased his overall points by 110. This made a dramatic difference to the courses open to him.

Entry to the colleges in the Central Applications Office (CAO) system is based on the points system. Students need to be able to present their six best subjects in the Leaving Certificate if they are to achieve their best possible points score.

Table 8.1: The Points System*

Leaving Cert. grade	Higher level	Ordinary level	Bonus**
A1	100	60	40
A2	90	50	35
B1	85	45	30
B2	80	40	25
B3	75	35	20
C1	70	30	15
C2	65	25	10
C3	60	20	5
D1	55	15	
D2	50	10	
D3	45	5	

*The best six results are counted for points calculation.
**Bonus points for Higher Maths are awarded by the University of Limerick.

Another consideration in option choice at senior cycle is that colleges and courses may have specific entry requirements. It is necessary to know these requirements in order to ensure that students do not exclude themselves from any course in which they are interested by not having the necessary subjects. Senior students should keep a careers file that includes details of colleges and courses.

CAO colleges set minimum entry requirements. An example of this is the institutes of technology where there is an entry requirement of five D3s at ordinary level in the Leaving Certificate, which must include a pass in Maths and English or Irish for many of their courses.

The four colleges of NUI (UCC, UCD, UCG and Maynooth) specify six subjects, two at higher level, with a pass in English, Irish and a third language. NUI recognises the Irish exemption granted by the Department of Education and Science. It also grants an exemption in the third-language requirement to students with serious dyslexia. Applications for this exemption should be made prior to the student entering senior cycle and forms are available from NUI, 49 Merrion Square, Dublin 2.

As previously discussed, such exemptions are important for some students with dyslexia. In the competitive points race that exists for courses at CAO level, it is important for students to be able to maximise points by presenting their six best subjects. Some students with dyslexia may have poor achievement in languages. As a result it is possible that subjects such as English, Irish and the third language may be taken at ordinary level. They may have excellent abilities in other subjects. Without exemptions in the language requirements, a student may have to take nine subjects in the Leaving Certificate in order to have six higher level subjects. This imposes two additional burdens. Firstly, nine subjects is an excessive amount, particularly when the fact that these are students who have a diagnosed learning difficulty is taken into account. Secondly, the students have to take language subjects in which they may have to work much harder than their peers to achieve a pass mark.

Certain courses have specific entry requirements. These are often related to what students will be studying. Some examples of subject requirements include:

- Maths
  - Higher level Maths is essential for Engineering honours degrees and Actuarial Studies;
  - Ordinary level Maths is a minimum requirement for many courses in the institutes of technology.
- English
  - Higher level English is essential for Clinical Speech in TCD, Journalism in DCU and Communications in DCU;
  - Ordinary level English is required for a wide range of institute of technology courses.
- Science
  - Science/medical/paramedical courses require a science subject. TCD requires two sciences for some medical/paramedical courses. DIT requires higher level Chemistry for Dietetics.

Complete information on course requirements is available in the college brochures. These are available from the Admissions Office in each college. Each college also has a website that can be found through the CAO website (www.cao.ie).

In conclusion the criteria for choosing subjects for Leaving Certificate include:

- Students should have the essential subjects needed for the courses they may consider doing after Leaving Certificate;
- They should choose subjects that will be of interest to them and that they will enjoy. This helps with motivation. Logically these subjects would tally with the strengths shown in their profile of abilities;
- If they are interested in applying for courses in the CAO system, they should choose subjects that will give them the best examination grades to maximise points.

Choices in the State Examination System

Levels of examination of subjects

In the Junior Certificate, students take the core subjects of Irish (unless exempt), English, Maths, History, Geography, CSPE (Civic, Social and Political Education) and SPHE (Social, Personal and Health Education). They then take either three or four other subjects from option lines.

In the case of Irish, English and Maths, subjects are offered at three levels: Higher, Ordinary and Foundation. SPHE and CSPE are offered at one common level. The other subjects are offered at two levels: Higher and Ordinary.

Table 8.2: Grade structure at second-level

Grade	%
A	85+
B	70–84
C	55–69
D	40–54
E	25–39
F	10–24
NG	<10

In the Leaving Certificate examination, there is a further breakdown of grades into A1, A2, B1, B2, B3, C1, etc. At both Leaving and Junior Certificate, students have to achieve at least a grade 'C' on a higher level paper to obtain an Honour result. Any grade below a 'D' is a fail grade.

It is generally the case that if students wish to take a subject at higher level in the Leaving Certificate, they should take the subject at higher level in the Junior Certificate. At Leaving Certificate six subjects count for points. There are more points given for higher level subjects, so for a student who wishes to apply to the CAO system, it is advisable to take as many higher level subjects as possible in the Junior Certificate.

There is no foundation level English available at Leaving Certificate. There is foundation level Maths and Irish. Students who take Foundation Level English at Junior Certificate level and then go on to do the traditional Leaving Certificate will face a huge jump in standard of English. If a student's English skills are so poor that foundation level at Junior Certificate is the appropriate level, it might be advisable to consider the Leaving Certificate Applied (LCA) as a route to Leaving Certificate.

Foundation level Maths at Junior Certificate is likely to lead on to foundation level Maths at Leaving Certificate. *Foundation level Maths is not acceptable for entry to many courses and careers.* The entry requirement for the vast majority of level six and seven courses in the institutes of technology is that the student should have five subjects in the Leaving Certificate including a 'D' in ordinary level English or Irish and in Maths. A decision that a student should take foundation level Maths might be made as early as second year. The student and parents often may not realise that the consequence of this decision is that the student is not eligible for entry to courses in the institutes of technology after Leaving Certificate. However, it is possible for a student to do a Post-Leaving Certificate Course (PLC) course and then apply to CAO colleges for entry based on the results of the PLC course.

Junior Certificate programmes

The Junior Certificate examination is the exam taken by the majority of second-level students. The Junior Certificate Schools Programme was introduced in 1996 for students whose particular needs were not adequately addressed in the broadly based Junior Certificate. The programme reaches out to young people who leave school early without obtaining any qualifications. The programme involves greater student activity and specific goals are set for literacy and numeracy. It is based on the concept that all young people are capable of achieving real success in school and that they can have a positive experience of education if the conditions are favourable. It is a way of working within the Junior Certificate programme that is specially designed to help young people who have had a difficult experience of school. Instead of examination grades, a student-profiling system is used to measure achievement. Details of the schools offering this programme are available from the Curriculum Development Unit, Sundrive Road, Dublin 12.

Leaving Certificate programmes

There are three types of Leaving Certificates programmes: the Leaving Certificate Applied Programme (LCA), the Leaving Certificate Vocational Programme (LCV) and the established Leaving Certificate Programme.

Leaving Certificate Applied (LCA) is a two-year self-contained programme. Its objective is to prepare participants for adult and working life. It has three main elements:

1. Vocational preparation, which focuses on preparation for work, work experience, enterprise and communications;
2. Vocational education, which gives students general life skills, including the arts, social education, leisure and languages;
3. General education, which is concerned with the development of mathematical, information technology and practical skills necessary for specialist areas such as tourism, business, horticulture, engineering or technology.

Students are assessed continuously throughout the two years. They receive credit for completing modules of the course and there are examinations at the end of the two years. After finishing the course, the students go on to employment or to PLC courses. They are not able to apply for CAO courses directly as the points system does not apply to the LCA. However, a student may proceed to a PLC course and then, on the basis of the PLC qualification, apply to the CAO colleges. The LCA was offered for the first time in 1996 in about 60 schools. In 2005 over 300 hundred schools offered it as a route to Leaving Certificate. The Department of Education and Science website (www.education.ie) has details of schools where it is offered.

The Leaving Certificate Vocational Programme (LCV) is a two year Leaving Certificate where the student takes the established Leaving Certificate with additional modules. Its objective is to strengthen the vocational dimension of the Leaving Certificate through relating and integrating specific pairings of subjects. The student takes a minimum of five subjects. These include Irish and a foreign language. Subjects that complement one another are grouped together and the student takes a particular group of subjects such as Engineering and Technical Drawing or Home Economics and Biology. There are link modules covering preparation for work, work experience and enterprise education to increase the vocational focus on the LCV. As students sit the established Leaving Certificate examination they can apply to CAO at the end of the LCV.

The established Leaving Certificate is one where students do a two-year course of study and there is an examination at the end of the two years. In some subjects such as Home Economics, Construction Studies and Engineering, there is a project or journal element. Most students take seven subjects. Subjects are offered at two levels, Higher and Ordinary. In Irish and Maths, Foundation level is also offered.

Future development of Senior Cycle

In 2003 the NCCA published a document called 'Developing Senior Cycle Education'. It was based on an extensive consultation process and discussed the direction developments in Senior Cycle may have taken by the year 2010. It was felt that the current examination puts too much stress on rote learning and places too much pressure on students. The proposals contained in the document looked towards a more adult learning culture, with a greater stress on self-directed learning. The NCCA stated the case for reform was clear. The current system was failing some 40 per cent of teenagers: 20 per cent perform poorly in the exam and a further 20 per cent drop out of the school system after Junior Certificate. It foresees the development of a different school culture in senior cycle. Some of the changes envisaged are as follows:

- Senior students will be involved in school organisation and policy and will have an input on the behaviour code, dress code and health policy in the school;
- There will be an emphasis on the development of skills and a reduction of content;

- The course will not be expressed as a list of topics but as outcomes broken into units. Examinations will take place mainly from January to June of the final year, though some will take place earlier;
- Assessment will be by written examination, oral/aurals, projects, assessment of group work and assessment of tasks. The majority of units will be externally assessed but there will be some school-based assessment.

In a letter to the NCCA in June 2005 the Minister for Education and Science, Mary Hanafin, indicated that while many of the changes were very welcome, further consideration should be given to some elements of the NCCA proposals. However, she backed a radical reform of the Leaving Certificate, which would see an earlier exam during the final school year as well as the June examinations. The earlier examinations would account for 25 per cent of the total marks: 'A second assessment in all subjects would have the benefit of reducing the much criticised stress imposed on students by a single high stakes terminal examination'.

From the NCCA document and the Minister's letter to the NCCA, change in the present structure of the Leaving Certificate is very likely by the year 2010.

Choices after the Junior Certificate

The majority of students decide to continue in education after the Junior Certificate and proceeds to one of the Leaving Certificate programmes. However, some students leave education after Junior Certificate. While they may enter into the workforce, it will generally be into low pay, low skill and frequently temporary employment. Many of these young people do not have the skills or resources to maintain any long-term position in the labour market. For those early school-leavers who do obtain employment there are significant differences in rates of pay between those who leave school with a Leaving Certificate and those who do not. Leaving school early will affect the life chances of students.

Options available to early school-leavers include:

Apprenticeship

Apprenticeship is the route to becoming a skilled craftsperson. The apprentice works for an employer in a chosen occupation and learns the necessary skills and knowledge. Apprenticeships are standard-based. This means apprentices must pass specific tests and assessments to ensure they meet certain pre-set standards of competency and skill. Apprenticeships comprise on-the-job training with the employer and off-the-job training in a FAS training centre or in an educational college.

The entry requirements for apprenticeships are that the applicant has reached sixteen years of age and has obtained a D grade in five subjects at Junior Certificate level. Although Junior Certificate is the minimum requirement for entry, most apprentices have a Leaving Certificate. Students with weaker literacy or numeracy skills may find it difficult to pass these tests/assessments and may require tutorial assistance from their college or training agency. Failure in these tests/assessments means that the apprenticeship cannot continue.

Youthreach

Young people who leave school without any qualification or with a Junior Certificate are the most vulnerable in the job market. Statistics show the highest unemployment and lowest wages are amongst this group. Youthreach is a special programme sponsored by the Department of Education and Science and the Department of Enterprise, Trade and Employment to give early school-leavers a second chance.

Youthreach offers young people an opportunity to gain qualifications and build self-confidence so they can move on into further education, training or work. It offers a range of qualifications including FETAC, City and Guilds and Junior and Leaving Certificates.

Employment

Most employment for early school leavers will be poorly paid, much of it part-time or temporary, with poor prospects of training or promotion.

The National Learning Network

The National Learning Network (www.nln.ie) is Ireland's largest non-government training organisation with 46 centres throughout

Ireland catering for over 2,000 students annually. There are no formal entry qualifications to any NLN course. Applicants must be over 16, be eligible for European Social Fund funding and be approved by the National Disability Authority. Applications from dyslexic students are considered for these courses

For the severely affected dyslexic student who is having enormous difficulty coping with the demands of second-level school, these courses provide a route to qualifications and skills. Courses are certified by outside examination bodies such as the Further Education and Training Awards Council (FETAC).

National Learning Network, in partnership with the Dyscovery Centre in Cardiff and the Institute of Technology, Blanchardstown, set up the National BUA centre in 2003. It provides assessment and support to people across the full spectrum of Specific Processing/Learning Difficulties (SPLDs) including dyslexia, dyspraxia (also known as DCD, Developmental Co-ordination Disorder), Asperger's Syndrome and Attention Deficit Hyperactive Disorder. Information on the centre is located on the NLN website.

Located on the campus of the Blanchardstown Institute of Technology, the National BUA Centre promotes inclusive education nationally through the development of a screening facility together with comprehensive educational, vocational and functional activity support services for third-level students and adult learners with specific processing/learning difficulties.

Choices after the Leaving Certificate

The choices after Leaving Certificate have improved for all students including those with dyslexia. There are more courses, more places on courses, new routes to qualifications and increased support services for students with dyslexia at third level.

The two main routes for students after Leaving Certificate are the CAO and PLC sectors.

Central Applications Office (CAO)

This is the application system for courses at honours degree, ordinary degree and higher certificate level in the universities, institutes of technology, nursing colleges and some other colleges. The closing date for applications is 1 February. Offers of places are determined by points, provided the student has satisfied the entry requirements of the college and any specific course requirements. The points from the previous year can be used as a rough guide but the points in any year are set by the number of applicants for a course and the number of places available.

In 2005 a new classification of courses in the CAO system was introduced. In the past, courses were called National Certificate, National Diploma and Degree. This has changed as follows:

Table 8.3: New classification of courses in CAO

Previous designation	New designation
National Certificate	Higher Certificate/level 6
National Diploma	Ordinary Degree/level 7
Degree	Honours Degree/level 8

On the application form students may list ten level eight courses and ten courses from levels seven and six, a total of twenty courses in all. It is essential that these are listed in order of preference.

Some points relevant to students with dyslexia:

- It is essential to research the colleges and courses thoroughly. It is necessary to acquire college brochures, attend open days and talk to the staff and students in the college.
- Consider the structure of the course. Continuous assessment is when assessments are graded throughout the year and the marks form part of the final grade for the year's work. Semesters mean that the year's work is divided into two semesters and examinations take place at the end of each semester. Both continuous assessment and semesters can help the student with dyslexia by spreading the academic demands throughout the year and reducing the amount to be memorised. Some courses in certain disciplines are taught through lectures and practicals, in which the student applies the knowledge learnt. This hands-on experience provides multi-sensory learning which suits many students with dyslexia. Other courses may be taught through reading lists and lectures. This may pose greater difficulty for such students.
- Use the CAO system fully. Do not restrict the choice to honours degrees/level eight. Use the level six and seven route as well. The CAO system is very flexible. Students may do a two-year higher certificate, transfer to an ordinary degree and then transfer to an honours degree if they obtain the necessary results.

- It is possible to apply for up to twenty courses. The courses must be listed in order of preference. Do not try to guess what the points may be. This leads to mistakes on the form.
- Consider courses outside the major cities. Frequently the same course has lower points in an institute of technology outside the major cities of Dublin, Cork, Limerick and Galway.
- Make sure to use the box on the form to indicate that you have a dyslexic difficulty. The CAO will send you out a form where you give details of the difficulty and the supports you may require at college. Such information cannot be used to your detriment. A recent psycho-educational assessment is necessary and must accompany the application for supports.

Support services for students at third level

The universities and the institutes of technology have a specific staff member whose responsibility it is to support students with disabilities. Disability officers work in the universities and access officers work in the institutes of technology. The role of the disability/access officer is to work collaboratively with students with disabilities in arranging supports that they may need while in college. Such supports may include assistive technology, examination arrangements, organising additional tuition or support during lectures.

The student accesses these supports by filling in the CAO form. On the first page of the form the question 'Do you have a Disability/ Specific Learning Difficulty?' appears. If the student indicates that a disability exists, the universities and institutes of technology to which the student is applying will be made aware of this. This does not disadvantage the applicant in any way. In March a supplementary information form is sent out to applicants who indicated that they had a disability. It is important to return the form by the return date which is set out on Page I of the form. One part of the form asks the student for information on the disability, the supports provided at second level and how school performance was affected. The student is free to add any further relevant information. The form must be accompanied by a second-level academic reference where the principal or guidance counsellor has to detail any adverse impact on the applicant's academic performance due to the disability and also state the supports provided for the student at second-level including accommodations in examinations. In the case of students with dyslexia, the form must be accompanied by a current psycho-educational assessment report. This is why it is important for a student entering senior cycle to have an updated assessment. The report is needed in March of the Leaving Certificate year. As there may be waiting lists of up to a year, arrangements for assessment should be made at the beginning of fifth year. In 2005 discussions were taking place among Disability Support Officers and Access Officers in order to set out criteria for the types of tests to be used in the assessment and the format of the report in order to establish the severity of the disability and the supports necessary.

AHEAD, the Association for Higher Education Access and Disability, is the organisation working to promote full access to and participation in third-level education for students with disabilities in Ireland and the website www.ahead.ie is a useful source of information.

Post-Leaving Certificate Courses (PLCs)

These courses are offered in colleges of further education. They are primarily designed to prepare students for the world of work and to develop vocational skills. While the majority are aimed at the ordinary level Leaving Certificate student who is unlikely to obtain a place in the CAO, some are in such specialised subjects that they could be a student's first choice regardless of CAO offers.

There is no central application process. Students apply directly to colleges. Many of the colleges have open days in February/March. Applications should be sent in from January on. Selection procedures differ and may include interviews, portfolios or aptitude tests.

There are increasing links between PLC courses and the colleges in the CAO system. This means that a student who achieves a good grade point average on a PLC course may apply and be considered for a course in the CAO system. Certification for PLC courses is provided by FETAC. In 2005 there are two schemes linking FETAC awards with entry to CAO. Details are on the website (www.fetac.ie).

The Higher Education Links Scheme links PLC courses to places in the universities mainly. There is a quota of places set aside for applicants. Allocation of places is decided on the basis of a grade point average on the eight modules of the PLC course. The PLC course must include modules that are linked to the course being applied for.

A Pilot Scheme was introduced in 2005 for applicants to the institutes of technology and some other higher education institutions. Applicants for level 6 and 7 courses may present results from any PLC course. Points are awarded for the 8 modules of the PLC course: 50 points for a distinction, 35 for a merit grade and 20 for a pass grade. This means that a student with 8 distinction grades gains 400 points and will compete with the cohort of Leaving Certificate students applying to the CAO on the basis of these points.

Disability support services are not as developed in the PLC sector as in CAO colleges. However, there is a partnership between the National Learning Network and City of Dublin Vocational Educational Committee (VEC) that offers a wide range of supports to students with disabilities in eight VEC colleges of further education in Dublin. These are Ballyfermot College of Further Education, Pearse College of Further Education, Inchicore College of Further Education, Colaiste Dhulaigh College of Further Education, Colaiste Ide College of Further Education, Plunkett College, Whitehall College of Further Education and Killester College of Further Education.

The partnership project currently has three full-time staff, which includes an Inclusive Education Project Co-ordinator and two Disability Support Officers. When students initially approach the service, the Disability Support Officer carries out a needs identification process with them to ensure they get the support they need in areas such as transport, assistive technology, benefits, class and study support and one-to-one tuition (visit www.nln.ie).

9. Coping at Second Level: Study Skills

This chapter is primarily addressed to students with dyslexia. It also should be of help to parents. At the beginning of second level, students may need help and guidance from parents in setting up study routines and establishing study methods. This chapter gives parents guidelines on how to help the student. As students mature, they should take increasing responsibility for their work, so that they become independent self-motivated learners by senior cycle. This is why the chapter is first and foremost directed to them.
  In it you will read about:

- The transition to second level;
- Organisation of time, study and work area;
- Accessing help;
- Study skills;
- Communicating information learnt;
- Examination strategies.

The Transition to Second Level

The change to second level is a big transition point for all students. Students go from having one teacher all day to having several teachers in the course of a day. There is the introduction of new subjects. There is more emphasis on examinations, both state and school-based. The school building is larger and there is far more movement as students move from class to class. Students may feel disorientated and lost as they try to find their way around. From being the biggest and oldest students at primary, they are now the smallest and youngest. The timetable for subjects each day differs and students need to be organised to have the correct books and/or homework ready on the right day.

The majority of students cope well, are very positive about the move and have settled in well by mid-term of first year. However, this transition may bring more pressures for students with dyslexia. The most obvious change is that at primary level students had one teacher who knew them and their difficulties well. Now they may face up to nine different teachers during the course of a single day. The pace at which information is passed on becomes faster as subject teachers have to complete courses in time for exams.

Parental support is critical at the start of second level so students make a successful transition from primary school. There is a major challenge in coping with all the new subjects, new teachers and the new structure of the school week. If they do not achieve some level of success, there is a risk that, as a defence mechanism, they may turn off the idea of school. Parents can help by communicating with each teacher the profile of the student's strengths and weaknesses and in asking the teacher about how they can best support the student at home. Parents can help with the organisation of homework, setting up routines for students that, over time, will become part of their study habits.

The following sections give guidelines on study skills for students or for parents who are helping them.

Organisation of Time, Work and Workplace

- Have a legible copy of the timetable in the front of the homework notebook so it can be referred to easily. It is useful if this is colour coded for the different subjects.

- Do homework at a regular time each day, preferably as early as possible. Again, at the weekend, try to do homework on Friday night or Saturday morning, leaving the rest of the weekend free.
- Schools give guidelines for the amount of time to be spent on homework. Students in first year, on average, would be expected to do about an hour and half to two hours a night. This includes written homework, learning homework and revision. This increases as students proceed through second level. Students with dyslexia often have to concentrate harder than other students. Short breaks of about five minutes during the study time help with concentration.
- Alternate subjects, beginning with a subject you like, followed by a subject you dislike.
- Have clear targets. Often the teacher will set such goals in homework assignments. However, students may need to organise their own revision work for exams. Targets should be specific and quantified. An example of such targets would be:
  - Learn five causes of coastal erosion;
  - Learn three examples of imagery in a poem with a quotation to illustrate each.
- It may be more difficult for students with dyslexia to cram before an exam. It can lead to confusion and the feeling of being overwhelmed. Therefore work consistently throughout the term.
- Have one homework notebook in which to enter all homework assignments, project dates, examination schedules and deadlines. It should be used to check that all homework is done and to pack the schoolbag for the following day.
- If you do not understand the homework set, ask the teacher for clarification at the end of class.
- Study/homework should be done at a desk, in a quiet and comfortable environment. Mobile phones should be switched off, as they can be a major source of distraction and are time-wasting. Equipment and books should be easily accessible. Good lighting should be in place. Keep a calendar close to the desk.
- Having a locker in school can lead to problems with books/equipment being left in school or at home. You need to develop a good checking procedure to see this does not happen. Having two sets of basic equipment such as pens, rulers etc. will minimise such difficulties. Colour coding can be used by putting stickers on subject text books and copies, for example red for Maths. Coloured folders could be used for the notes in different subjects.

- At the beginning of a lesson, get everything you need ready on the desk so that you do not waste time.

Accessing Help

- In the early years of secondary school, it is likely to be your parents who ensure that teachers are aware of the learning difficulties. Schools are very busy places. Teachers deal with several hundred students in a week. It is easy to overlook the needs of an individual student. Parents should send in a summary of the assessment to each teacher at the beginning of the school year. They should not assume that if they inform the principal or another teacher that this information will be passed on to the other staff automatically.
- As you mature and understand more about how you learn, you can provide information to teachers on techniques that help you learn. The CD ROM/DVD *Understanding Dyslexia* has a self-help section. It helps students understand dyslexia and how it affects them. It assists in analysing individual learning profiles. It also includes a self-help questionnaire that helps students inform teachers about what they can do to help the individual student. The questionnaire gets students to analyse what teachers do that the students like and what teachers could do to help them learn better. This provides a format for such information to be given to teachers diplomatically. This CD ROM is in the school. Ask if you may borrow a copy of it.
- Sometimes students may encounter a teacher who is not aware of the range of difficulties that a student with dyslexia may have. Be prepared: have information on the topic to hand out and then be ready to explain how you are affected. This is good preparation for third level and working life, where you may have to explain dyslexia to others.

Study Skills

- Successful learning does take effort. However, it becomes easier the more the techniques are practised. Material must be gone over several times to ensure it is remembered. Rewriting notes, taping and reading aloud are all ways to help memory. There are websites that may help develop study skills such as www.skoool.ie and www.learnforsuccess.info.

- It is easier to learn material that is understood. Ask for help if you do not understand what has been taught in class.
- Keep a vocabulary notebook in each subject for the new words and their specific meanings in that subject.
- If you learn more effectively by listening in class, sit near the front of the classroom and close to students who want to learn.
- Students who miss a lot of school tend to be low achievers. Students with dyslexia usually have more difficulty catching up on missed classes and so it is important to attend school regularly.
- Do homework as thoroughly as possible. This is part of the learning process.
- It is relatively easy for a teacher to check on written homework and so students often make written homework a priority. However, it is the learning homework that is important for success in exams. Many students believe that if they read over a text several times, they know it. Unfortunately this is not the case. They need to actively learn the material and then have a checking process to make sure it is learnt. Techniques such as note-taking help with this.
- Some students with dyslexia may find it very difficult to summarise material in textbooks and make their own notes. This can be due to poor or slow reading where they may have to reread a piece several times to see the points the writer is making, difficulties in summarising and organising material or difficulties in the presentation of legible and clearly laid-out notes. The essential task is to learn the information. Having to make their own notes from the text can place additional barriers in their way. These students can therefore benefit hugely from getting precise and concise notes.
- Revision handbooks are a useful way to access the key points in the different subjects and could be used from first year on. They are available from a number of educational publishers in a range of subjects at Junior and Leaving Certificate level. The website www.skoool.ie contains study notes on most subjects in the Junior Certificate and Leaving Certificate.
- If teachers dictate their own notes to the class, it can be a problem for students with dyslexia because of difficulties in processing language and in spelling and handwriting. These students will find it challenging to listen and write at the same time. If necessary, the teacher should arrange for photocopies of notes to be given to students. These could be photocopies of teacher notes or the notes of a student who makes well-organised, legible notes.

- Some students feel that once the notes are made and filed that the work is done. Notes must be learnt. This learning can be checked by an oral recital or writing them out again. Memory techniques such as chunking information together and mnemonics may help with learning. Mnemonics are techniques to help memory. An example is that to remember the four factors of production – capital, enterprise, land and labour – the student makes up a word, *CELL*, which comprises the first letter of each word.

- If you are an aural rather than a visual learner, tapes of notes and/or texts can be helpful. You may benefit from repeating material to be learnt aloud or reading drafts of essays aloud to see if they make sense. Co-operative learning might help if a small group of friends studies together and tests each other.

- You may have a strong visual memory. This can be used when learning. You may be able to recall the look of a page of notes. This assists in the recall of the content of the page. Make use of colour, numbering of points, margins, headings and diagrams when making notes. A mindmap is a technique that helps students organise and summarise information. It can be used for note-taking or for planning essays. The CD ROM *Understanding Dyslexia* has a section on mindmaps.

- You may have difficulty in deciphering the meaning of complex texts, having to reread pages several times to make sense of the material. It can be helpful to make notes showing the development of the points in the text.

- Ask a teacher prior to a class for the notes or a copy of the overhead slides that will be used. It means less writing and you can listen and concentrate on what is said. The structure and sequence of the lecture is clearly laid out. It is also possible to include additional notes or points where relevant.

- If you find you cannot read the textbooks quickly or well enough to understand the content, ask someone such as a parent or sister/brother to read the text aloud so you can concentrate on listening. Certain computer programmes scan and read text aloud as the words appear on the screen.

- When reading, use a highlighter to mark important parts of the text.

Communicating Information Learnt

- Before beginning an assignment, check you understand what you are being asked to do.

- Presentation and layout can help teachers understand written assignments, so try to improve the legibility of handwriting and ensure that headings and question numbers are clearly indicated. In Maths, numbers should be aligned correctly so mistakes will not be made.
- If you have great difficulty with written homework, ask teachers if they would accept alternatives such as taped or typed homework.
- If you will be using reasonable accommodations in state examinations, you should be able to use similar accommodation in house examinations. You need to become familiar with the relevant type of accommodation and practise it.
- Become computer literate as soon as possible, preferably early at second level. Computers are of enormous help to students with dyslexia: they help with presentation, spelling, grammar and editing.
- Some students with dyslexia have difficulty seeing and organising patterns. Good notes are an effective way to see the structure of what you are learning. The notes are a useful device in organising material and are helpful in formatting your own answers. Because the notes are structured, you can use that structure when answering questions.

Examination Strategies

- As you proceed through second level, organising course material for revision becomes increasingly important. Make out a master sheet showing all the topics to be covered in each subject. Have a timetable where each subject is revised two or three times a week. When a topic has been revised, mark it off on the master sheet. Monitoring the progress you are making in revising the subjects will help with exam anxiety.
- A revision plan sets out a timetable where the subject is revised on a frequent basis. Such a plan could entail learning the material on the night of the lecture, a weekly revision of all new material learnt and a monthly revision of the month's work. Each revision should take a shorter time.
- Have copies of the exam timetable in prominent places showing the date, time and place of the examination.
- Check you have the correct equipment for each examination. Ensure you have spares for essential equipment, for example spare batteries for the calculator.

- Prior to the exam, make sure you are familiar with the examination format and how marks are allocated. Also make sure you understand the words used in examinations. Words such as *describe, analyse, classify, contrast, evaluate and define* describe very precise tasks. Use past examination papers to help you.
- Allocate a time for each question. If you find yourself running out of time, use bullet points to show the information that you have not had time to complete. Leave space between the points, so that if you have time at the end to return to the question, you can add in extra information.
- Make sure you have a watch so you can be aware of your timing. Be careful not to make the classic mistake of spending more than your allotted time on one or two questions to the neglect of others. If you only do two out of five questions that have equal marks, no matter how well you have answered, you can only obtain a maximum of 40 per cent.
- Take time to read the paper thoroughly, making sure you understand each part of the question. Mark the questions you intend to answer. Start with a question to which you are fairly confident you know the answer.
- Underline the key words in a question and answer that question. Marks are not given for writing down all you know about a subject. The information needs to be relevant to the question asked.
- Remember to number questions and parts of questions clearly. Drawings should be labelled precisely.
- Do every step of a question. Do not take shortcuts. In subjects such as Maths and Business Studies, you get marks for the correct method, even if the final answer is wrong. If you skip some steps, it is easier to go wrong. Also, some marking schemes give marks for showing the workings of the answer.
- Make sure you answer all parts of a question. If the question asks for three points, you need to make three points. Otherwise you lose marks.
- Proofread the whole paper once it is completed, if you have time. Double-check calculations.
- It can be very useful to analyse returned examination papers to see where you lost marks. Make out an analysis grid where the marks allocated for each part of each question are set out and then enter the mark you obtained and work out what percentage you achieved. This allows you to see the questions in which you did well and where you lost marks.

10. Dyslexia at Second Level: Supports and Strategies

This chapter is primarily addressed to second-level schools and teaching staffs. It is well recognised by professionals working in the field of education that while there have been major advances in understanding dyslexia and provision of supports at both primary and third level, the second-level sector in Ireland has not made similar progress. Because of this fact the chapter is also addressed to parents to inform them about the possible supports and teaching strategies that should be available in schools. It means they are well informed when discussing school-based supports with the school. It may also be possible to circulate the information and suggestions to teachers.

The topics covered in the chapter include:

- Sources of information about dyslexia for teachers;
- The whole-school approach;
- School support structures;
- Teaching study skills;
- Communication with the student;
- Access to subject content;
- Communication of information learnt;
- Dyslexia-friendly schools.

As part of the training on the new curriculum at primary level, all teachers receive in-service training on the topics of special education. The improvement in services for students with dyslexia and other difficulties at third level has been the result of the development of the Disability Support Service in the colleges. However, at second level the majority of serving teachers have received little or no in-service or pre-service training on the topic of dyslexia or special needs. This absence of training has resulted in underdeveloped services and a lack of knowledge about teaching strategies in this sector of education.

This point is illustrated by a survey of the second-level students who attended the DAI AGM in 2005. Forty students completed the questionnaire. The findings include the following:

- 45 per cent of the students had to look after their own needs such as getting notes, organising a reader for examinations or placing a desk near a power point for a laptop. A further 30 per cent had to do this sometimes;
- In 25 per cent of the schools represented by the students it was the school who took the responsibility to inform the teachers of the student's difficulties. Otherwise it was the parents or students themselves who had to inform teachers;
- 47.5 per cent of the students felt teachers need to get informed about dyslexia. Overall students felt teachers did not understand dyslexia and the difficulties students experience in the classroom. One student made the comment that older teachers did not care but that the younger teachers helped and cared more.

At second level there is continuing development of numeracy and literacy skills but there are new challenges to be faced. If students are to succeed in examinations they must be able to access subject content and then to communicate the knowledge learnt. It is only in language subjects that marks are deducted for spelling and grammar. Special needs teachers have an input on the development of literacy and numeracy skills if the student falls within the criteria for such help. Many students with dyslexia do not fall within such criteria. However, all students with dyslexia, whether they receive extra help or not, rely on the mainstream teacher for subject teaching. This means each teacher needs to understand how dyslexia affects students and the most appropriate teaching strategies and supports for students to reach their full potential.

The Task Force on Dyslexia recognised the key involvement of mainstream teachers both in identifying possible learning difficulties

arising from dyslexia and in addressing the needs of students identified as having such difficulties. It states that mainstream teachers
should assume major responsibility for the progress and development of each student in their classes who has learning difficulties
arising from dyslexia, with learning support and resource teachers
and other professionals assuming supporting roles. The Task Force
recommended that subject teachers 'provide differentiated instruction' to such students.

Differentiation is the process whereby teachers select appropriate teaching methods to match an individual student's learning
strategies within the class group. The Department of Education
and Science Inspectorate look for differentiation during subject
inspections. There are many ways it can be done. Here are some
examples:

- If the student has strong visual spatial ability, videos, tapes,
  drawings, diagrams or mindmaps could be used to present information, both by the teacher when teaching and the student when
  doing homework;
- Use multi-sensory teaching methods so that as many as possible of the student's senses are being stimulated;
- Adapt class and homework goals for individual students. For a
  student with writing difficulties, accept answers that are shorter
  than the class average, as it may take this student longer to produce the short answer.

Books such as *Dyslexia: Successful Inclusion in the Secondary
School* (Peer and Reid, 2003) give guidelines to teachers on ways
to differentiate in different subject areas. Tailoring teaching techniques to meet individual needs takes time and time is at a pre-
mium in the classroom. However, some of these students will fail to
achieve unless teachers are aware of their specific strengths and
needs, and use teaching methods that help them to achieve.

Sources of Information About Dyslexia for Teachers

- The video/CD ROM/DVD *Understanding Dyslexia* is a joint initiative of the Departments of Education in Ireland, North and South
  that was issued to all schools in 2005. It is an invaluable source
  of information and includes sections on the psychological assessment, teaching strategies at primary and post-primary and advice
  for parents. The resources section on the CD ROM/DVD includes

extensive and comprehensive information on books, tests, ICT material and websites. Highlighted in the section for post-primary teachers is the following definition of fairness.

> To successfully manage the inclusive classroom, teachers should re-examine the notion of what is 'fair'. 'Fair' does not mean every pupil gets the same treatment but that every pupil gets what he or she needs. Equity should be promoted in every classroom.

- The psychological assessment may include a profile of the student's learning strengths and needs as well as practical suggestions about appropriate teaching strategies. If teachers have difficulty understanding the terminology used in the assessment, the CD ROM provides a guide to its interpretation.
- Students and parents are also a source of information about techniques that work or do not work. Parents may have been involved from an early age in providing support for homework and may be very familiar with the student's difficulties.
- The CD ROM *Understanding Dyslexia* has a self-help questionnaire for the student. The purpose of this is to help students analyse how they learn and which teaching strategies help. Asking the student such questions can be a very effective part of an evaluation of teaching strategies by the teacher.
- Each school should have a communication process so that every mainstream teacher is informed of a student's profile, highlighting the strengths and needs. This should be done in September of each school year and at regular intervals during the year. Information on which students are availing of accommodations in examinations should be passed on.
- Under the Education of Persons with Special Educational Needs Act 2004 there is an obligation that individual education plans (IEPs) are in place for students with special needs. Under the Learning Support Guidelines 2000, individual pupil learning programmes (IPLPs) should be prepared for students qualifying for learning support teaching. It is recommended that these plans and programmes are drawn up on a whole-school approach involving mainstream teachers, the learning support and resource teacher, the parents and the pupil themselves.
- Each school should build up a library of relevant texts for teachers. There are an increasing number of books becoming available on practical strategies for teachers in different subject areas at second level. The book *Dyslexia: Successful Inclusion in the Secondary School* (Peer and Reid, 2003) has chapters dedicated to

teaching in subject areas such as Physics, Biology, Maths, History, Geography, Art and Music, English and foreign languages. Again, the CD ROM/DVD *Understanding Dyslexia* has an extensive list of resources and books.

- Students may still come into second level with undiagnosed dyslexia. All teachers need to be aware of the indicators so that they are able to refer the student for further investigation. The Task Force report included four lists of indicators depending on the age of the child. There is a list of indicators for the age 12+, which is the appropriate list for second level. All teachers need a copy of these indicators for reference purposes. They are available in the Task Force Report, on the CD ROM/DVD *Understanding Dyslexia* and in Chapter 2.

The Whole-School Approach

Under the Education Act 1998, schools are required to have a school plan which sets out the steps the school is taking to ensure equality of access and participation, and that appropriate education will be provided for students. The Education of Persons with Special Educational Needs Act 2004 sets out the right of the child with special needs to an inclusive education in mainstream schooling.

A whole-school approach is essential, as all teachers have a role in achieving these goals. The principal and deputy principal have responsibilities in defining school policy, delegating responsibilities of meeting such policy to teachers, allocating resources and ensuring that teachers have sufficient training. Year heads and tutors need to know about the student's needs. Guidance counsellors have a key role in helping the student make informed educational choices. Mainstream teachers play a key role as they provide access to the curriculum. Even if students qualify for resource or learning support, it is only for a limited amount of time. The student spends the majority of the school day with the mainstream teacher.

Many students with mild/moderate dyslexia may not qualify for learning support/resource teaching. The school plan should clearly state the person responsible for ensuring they receive the necessary supports. They may need only minimum interventions, such as assessment and provision of reasonable accommodation or application for the NUI third-language exemption. A named teacher needs to be responsible.

It is through whole-school approaches that most success can be achieved. If a student is taught to do a task in one subject and can apply this knowledge in other subject areas, it provides for over-learning. An example is learning to draw graphs in Maths. The same methods can be used to draw graphs in other subject areas such as Geography or Business. Students can become confused if teachers in different subject areas differ in approach to tasks that are similar.

School Support Structures

- When a student is exempt from Irish, is it possible to use this class time positively? It could be used for extra tuition, extra computer time or extra English reading.
- Is a teacher allocated the responsibility for ensuring all the teachers are informed about students with difficulties on a regular basis?
- There should be a school policy on screening and identification. All teachers should have a copy of the list of indicators from the Task Force Report. There should be forms available so they could refer students for further investigation by the guidance counsellor or special needs teachers.
- If there is streaming, does it take account of the student with dyslexia who may be very intelligent and articulate but who has verbal difficulties?
- A common profile of students with dyslexia is stronger Maths/technical abilities and weaker verbal abilities. In a streamed situation will these students be able to access an appropriate level of Maths tuition?
- Is there positive discrimination in the allocation of option subjects? Do students have to study a foreign language?
- Has the school ensured that teachers have received in-service training on learning difficulties? The Special Education Support Service (SESS) provides such training for teachers. It also provides subsidies for courses (for details, visit www.sess.ie).

Study Skills

- Order and structure may need to be taught, as these skills do not come naturally to some students with dyslexia. Students need to know how to file and organise work, manage equipment and books, use a watch and calendar, keep to timetables, manage the homework notebook, manage time and meet deadlines, and prioritise tasks.

- Some students have difficulty remembering sequences such as days of the week or months of the year. A personal diary where all appointments, timetables and work assignments can be entered is helpful.
- Training in effective reading skills will enable the student to become a far more efficient reader. These skills are developed by asking students to survey the material before beginning a reading task, to ask themselves what they might learn and then to read to find the answers to these questions. The student should then review what they learnt in order to help retain the information.
- Training in study skills helps students organise their work. Clear instructions about standards of written work, such as layout and length of answer expected should be given. Guidelines about points to be included in the answer can help to ensure enough is written. Some students have little idea about the techniques involved in learning work. Techniques in note-taking, goal setting, improving memory and checking of material learnt need to be taught.
- Prior to exams, students may require help in setting up a revision plan. Because of working memory difficulties they may panic coming up to an examination when they have to remember a lot of information. They should concentrate on learning with understanding and not to rote learn. These are students who should avoid cramming and who should work at a consistent pace throughout the year.

Communication with the Student

- Check if the student is willing to read aloud. Some would prefer to do so and not be treated differently from the rest of the class. Others are very conscious that their reading skills are laboured and this anxiety can make their reading worse. Do not ask them to read unless it is essential. If that is the case, show them what they will have to read in advance so that they can practice it at home prior to the class.
- Break down instructions into simple commands. Do not give an instruction that is a complicated sequence, for example 'After you

have taken down your homework and before you leave the room, clean the desk'. Break it down to a series of shorter commands. Emphasise the points that are important, by repetition if necessary.

- Give written notices of events, timetables, written assignments and exam dates.
- When correcting, be sparing in the use of red pen. Not all mistakes need to be marked. Take a particular category of error and correct it. There is a greater chance that the student will learn from this. A comment such as, 'Improve your writing' has little effect on the standard of writing. The student may not know how to improve handwriting. Try to identify one fault which can be worked on, for example suggesting the student close the loops in letters such as a, d, g. If the idea is right, give marks regardless of spelling, layout and presentation. Many of the students will qualify for a waiver of spelling and grammar in state examinations.
- Write clearly on the board, preferably in print. Give plenty of time for information to be taken down. A student with dyslexia may find this task difficult. If the student has major difficulties accessing information from the board, are there other methods of passing on this information?
- Worksheets should be written simply, with large print and clear spacing.

Access to Subject Content

- Multi-sensory teaching can help learning. If lessons include written, oral and visual elements, these provide more hooks for the student to remember the content. For this reason, use of audio tapes, videos and DVDs may be helpful. Charts and diagrams can make it easier for the student to visualise information and can act as a summary, making the task of learning easier.
- The student may have great difficulty in deciphering script handwriting whether it is on the board, in notes or on exam papers. Teacher notes and test papers are best typed.
- Students may have difficulty taking legible notes due to poor handwriting, layout and spelling. Give them copies of your own notes. If this is not possible, photocopies of other students' notes can be helpful.
- Some students may not understand what it is they are being asked to do in a question. It is important that they are taught how questions are structured and the precise meanings of words used in questions.

- Be conscious of the readability of texts. Many Junior Certificate texts use English aimed at students with reading ages in the mid-teens. Sentences may be lengthy and use several clauses. The vocabulary used may contain new words. As a result the information contained may be inaccessible for students who do not have this level of reading skills. Students need access to the content of the subject in order to learn. The use of revision handbooks may provide access to the key points.
- When reading textbooks, introduce the content so students become tuned in to the gist of the material and keywords. This will help with comprehension. If it is a text with questions at the end of sections, get students to read the questions before reading the text, so they know what points are relevant.
- Provide a list of vocabulary for a new topic and check the student understands these words.
- Display keywords and formulae around the walls of the classroom.
- Some students have difficulty recalling the name of an object or person. A student may know all about Leonardo Da Vinci and yet have difficulty recalling his name. Such students should overlearn the names of people and objects. One method of doing this is to use vocabulary notebooks that contain the new words and names in each subject. These can form the basis for revision just before an exam, as it is these words that may be most difficult to recall in the exam. Such a notebook will also help if spelling is a problem. Encourage students to learn the spellings in this notebook.
- Make sure the student has a picture of the course being covered. When introducing new work, give an overview of the topic. It can help the student see the structure and can draw the different strands together.
- Maths teachers need to be aware of the specific difficulties students with dyslexia may have in Maths. Students need to know the language and symbols used in Maths.

Communication of Information Learnt

- When given questions to answer orally in class, some students have difficulty processing the question asked, retrieving the information and structuring what they want to say. These difficulties can be compounded by anxiety and frustration. Teachers can help by giving extra time or by having a specific arrangement when they ask a particular student a question.

- Some students may find it difficult to understand the structure of a question. As a result their answers may be off the point and they therefore lose marks. Show students how to analyse the question, breaking it down into its constituent parts. Make sure they are familiar with the nuances of the language used in questions.
- Give a structure for attempting longer written answers. Too often answers are too short because they lack structure. Students need to be trained to plan answers before starting to write. Mindmaps are a very useful technique here.
- Because students may have difficulty with written work, consider other means of collecting and presenting information such as tapes or word processors. Multiple choice questions, worksheets or visual presentations by way of diagrams all help the student show what they know.
- Students may be granted some accommodations in state examinations, which can lead to a significant difference in their results. Students need training in the use of appropriate accommodation and can benefit in presenting homework and sitting house exams using the accommodation.
- Be understanding when giving poetry or other sequences to be learnt off by heart. Due to memory difficulties some students may find it exceptionally difficult to remember a sequence regardless of how much time they spend on the task.

Dyslexia-Friendly Schools

The dyslexia-friendly school is a concept pioneered by the British Dyslexia Association (BDA) and has been embraced by many schools and Local Education Authorities (LEAs) throughout the UK and in the USA. A BDA Quality Mark has been introduced which promotes inclusion through dyslexia-friendly LEAs and schools. Progress is being made to introduce the concept in Northern Ireland. The initiative aims to identify, promote and celebrate excellent practice in improving access to learning for children. Part of the reason it has been so successful is that the changes that make schools more dyslexia friendly also lead to more effective schools for all students.

The British Dyslexia Association has published a resource pack, *Achieving Dyslexia Friendly Schools*. It states that LEAs are beginning to report improvements in key indicators of effectiveness such as:

- Attendance;
- Performance in examinations;
- Pupil confidence, self-esteem and behaviour;
- Parental confidence;
- Teacher confidence following whole-school training.

LEAs are also beginning to report reductions in exclusions and appeals.

The concept of dyslexia friendly means that the school culture would include some of the following characteristics:

- Gardner's Theory of Multiple Intelligences, which suggests there are at least seven intelligences, each with its own preferred way of learning. Everyone possesses varying degrees of each of these intelligences. Teachers who ensure that class instruction is structured to use the different learning preferences of students empower more students to be successful in their learning;
- A supportive environment where the learner feels safe and supported and where teachers make it clear that it is okay to be dyslexic;
- Clear guidelines about tasks, what is to be achieved and how it will be assessed with positive feedback from teachers including constructive comments on how improvements can be made;
- Setting achievable goals is crucial to the self-esteem of the student;
- Empowering students by allowing them discuss what helps and what does not help;
- Teacher self-evaluation.

11. Dyslexia and Mathematics

This chapter will be of use to parents and teachers. In it you will read about:

- Maths difficulties that may affect students with dyslexia;
- How parents can help the student in Mathematics;
- A brief guide for teachers including sources of information on teaching Mathematics to students with dyslexia.

Difficulties with Mathematics

Many people believe that dyslexia affects spelling, reading and handwriting. It may take parents by surprise when achievement in Maths is also affected. These mathematical difficulties may vary considerably from the child who verges on dyscalculia (having extreme difficulty with Maths concepts and calculations) to students who have good or superior ability in Maths but whose dyslexia may hold them back in some way.

The types of difficulty that may affect the mathematical achievement of students include:

- Students may not be able to read the English in the question and therefore may not know what task they are being asked to do.
- Confusion about the vocabulary used in Maths and the exact meaning of words. Words such as *equal*, *product* and *add* have exact meanings in Maths that may not be the same as their everyday meaning. The words *write* and *right* can be particularly confusing with all the varied meanings the same sound can convey. These varied meanings include:
  - The opposite of wrong;
  - The opposite of left;
  - Correct;
  - To write down;
  - A right angle of 90 degrees.
- The use of different words to describe the same mathematical action. An example is the instruction for adding: the words *add, increase, plus* and *total* may be used. It is no wonder some students get confused.
- Students may not understand the instructions given by the teacher. This may be because the teacher uses different words to those in the text. It could also result from students having difficulty following the sequence of instructions given verbally due to short-term memory difficulties. Lack of confidence may compound this difficulty, as students may be hesitant in asking questions.
- In textbooks some questions are phrased such that information is put in a different sequence to the actions the student is required to take. For example, 'John has 46 cents. He wants to buy a bar that costs €1. How much more does he need'? A more straightforward way of putting this question is to ask, 'A bar costs €1. John has 46 cents. How much more does he need'? This

follows the sequence of the task and the child understands it more easily.

- Students may not be clear on the meaning of the symbols used in Maths. Many students with dyslexia show a weakness in the coding subtest in the psycho-educational assessment. This means they may find symbols confusing. Students with spatial or directional confusion may even find it difficult to distinguish between the symbol + and x.
- Sequencing and short-term memory difficulties may mean that learning tables becomes a marathon task. Frequently, students would be able to do complicated Maths tasks if they could remember their tables.
- Poor organisation and layout on the page may result in numbers not being aligned correctly, with figures squashed together so that it is difficult to read them or lines which have not been drawn with a ruler so the page looks untidy.
- Poor writing skills, such that numbers are not clear and are mis-read, thus leading to the wrong answer. Other students, due to poor hand–eye co-ordination, find it difficult to draw lines, measure angles and even use a ruler competently. Some may still reverse numbers.
- There may be confusion about place value, so the student may confuse tens, hundreds and thousands. This confusion is increased when decimal points are involved.
- Sequential memory difficulties can mean some students may remember fewer numbers in their heads than the average student. This slows down the speed of processing. Some students may find it very difficult to count backwards.
- Some students need to decipher mental arithmetic sums in order to visualise the question and then process the answer. This slows down answering.
- Left/right difficulties. In Maths the student usually works from right to left, which is opposite to the way words are read. For students with spatial/directional difficulties this adds to the confusion.
- Different learning styles. Some students do not show the workings of problems, but often appear to have the right answer without knowing how they got there.

These difficulties result in students underperforming in Maths and possibly disliking the subject. Maths is a sequential subject, where each lesson is based on previous learning. If students have not acquired the earlier skills for some reason, they may have difficulty in understanding the current work in class.

As students proceed through the school system, the verbal content of the subject lessens. At the same time reading stamina and skills are developing. This may mean that students who had difficulty with understanding the language of Maths or deciphering questions may find more success at second level. Therefore it is important to have an accurate assessment of the child's potential to ensure informed decisions are made about the appropriate level at which the student will study Maths.

At second level, Maths is taught at three levels for the Junior and Leaving Certificate. These levels are Higher, Ordinary and Foundation. If students are capable of taking the higher level paper, they need to be studying it from first year. Dropping to ordinary level may have career implications later on. An example is that a 'C' grade in higher level Maths at Leaving Certificate is a requirement for Engineering honours degrees at third level. In a school where classes are streamed, it might be the case that a student with dyslexia with good Maths skills, may be placed in one of the weaker classes on account of poorer verbal skills and higher level Maths is not taught in that class. Higher level Maths is a long and extensive course at all levels and the pace in these classes is very fast. A student who has not been in the higher level class in the early years of second level will find it very difficult, if not impossible, to catch up at a later stage.

Taking foundation level Maths may have major implications when a student is applying for courses after second level, as it is not accepted as an entry requirement of the institutes of technology. More detailed information about entry requirements is presented in Chapter 8.

The difficulties listed at the beginning of this chapter may mean that the entrance assessment for second level may not give a realistic indication of the student's potential in Maths. If there are questions expressed as problems in English and the child cannot read the question, it is more a test of the child's English than Maths. Some assistance at entrance assessment should be part of the support services provided by schools. This could include the reading of the questions and the provision of a calculator or tables square.

How Parents can Help

There are many ways parents can help the child develop number skills from an early age. Many of the ideas below can be incorporated in play and everyday activities. They could become part of daily routine, such as each time children brush their teeth they count the strokes or each time a cake is cut it is divided into halves, then quarters and eighths. A word of caution, however: parents only have so much energy so it is important that such activities are relaxed and fun, that the effort expended does not exhaust the parent and that the child does not perceive the activities as more work. The most important contribution parents can make is a stable loving relationship. Many of the activities below build on this relationship but if parents are exhausted and tired, patience can be one of the casualties. Therefore, choose activities that seem most relevant at a particular stage for the child. Be consistent and build them into the daily or weekly routine. Do not try to do everything.

Possible activities to encourage numeracy include:

- Encourage the development of hand skills through drawing and colouring tasks. This is a natural stage of development when the child is very young. It may help if it is encouraged to continue through middle childhood. Use of rulers and other drawing games, such as Spirographs, helps develop better hand control.
- Play family games that help develop an understanding of number. Many card games help with number skills. Games such as Ludo and Snakes and Ladders may help develop counting skills and an understanding of concepts such as up/down and counting backwards.
- Songs and nursery rhymes help with the memorising numbers and days of the week, while making the activity fun.
- Ask the child to read the bus, train or ferry timetables when travelling.
- Simple household tasks can be used to provide examples of mathematical concepts. Cut a pizza into halves and then quarters and eighths, and use the terminology of fractions when giving out slices.
- Use car journeys to help the child work out a sense of distance. Get them to watch the speedometer and ask them to estimate how long the journey will take. Keep a record of the distance travelled and how long it took.
- The younger child could count the steps in the stairs.
- When shopping, ask the child to pick items from the shelves and check the weight or volume.
- Parents can help develop a sense of time that can include the hours, months and seasons. Put up cards showing the important times during the day and then ask children to read the clock to confirm the time. Suggest children read the TV guide to pick out programmes to watch and then use the clock to identify the time.

Enter future events in a calendar on the wall. Get them to work out how long it is until a birthday or other celebration. Help the older child use the homework notebook as an aid to see the routine of the week and term, and to check that the right books and homework for the different school days are in the schoolbag.

- Play games with young children that involve counting using items such as buttons or dolls. This means that they have a multi-sensory approach, which helps give them a concrete concept of number.

- If there are particular symbols or words causing problems, put them on cards so the child sees them regularly. These cards could then be used as a bookmark or put up on the fridge.

- Do not help them so much with homework that it becomes mainly your own work. The teacher needs to know if they have difficulty doing the tasks set. If the homework is presented with the right answers, it means the teacher may overestimate their ability in the subject. However, there are practical ideas for helping:
  - If the child does not understand the question, read it aloud, maybe putting the question in simpler language, so that the mathematical task is understood.
  - Provide them with number squares or calculators so their lack of knowledge of tables does not hold them back.
  - Use direction arrows and colour coding for the different mathematical operations.
  - Make sure they have the proper equipment. Maths copies with pages made out in squares help presentation and they should use a square for every number. When doing fractions they should not try to squash the fraction into one square but use a square for each number, even if it appears to use a lot of space. Pens with padded grips can help if their grip on the pencil is very tight. Rulers should be used for anything that requires the drawing of a straight line. Show them how to lay their work out with plenty of space so it does not end up squashed up in the corner of the page.
  - Listen to them and try to identify their difficulty. Could it be the English in the questions, the inability to remember tables or the inability to hold a series of numbers in their head? The latter makes mental arithmetic difficult. As parents, you are with the child on a one-to-one basis more often than anyone else and you are more likely to observe such problems. Pass any observations on to the school.
  - Give students time to rest. They make more mistakes when tired and may find it more difficult to understand a concept.

A change to another subject or a short break for something to eat may boost energy.
- Help them develop the technique of estimating answers. Use concrete examples such as, 'If you have €20.00 and buy a CD for €9.99, roughly how much change will you have?' Encourage them to round it to €10 for a rough answer.
- If writing numbers backwards is a difficulty, have a card close to their working area with the numbers clearly shown so they can refer to it.
- Some children may look at a Maths question and work out the answer in their heads. Writing down the interim steps in reaching that answer seems like too much hard work. However, it is necessary to develop the step-by-step approach for several reasons. Firstly, the Maths will become more difficult and they need to be accustomed to writing down each stage. This teaches them a methodical approach, which will benefit their maths and also have a knock-on effect in other subjects. Secondly, marks in examinations are allocated to the stages of working out answers. If a child follows the correct procedure and gets the answer wrong, they still get marks for the correct method. The child who does not show the working out of problems will get zero for a wrong answer.
- Many children understand the concept when taught in class and are able to do the homework that night. However, over time, they can lose that understanding. Regular revision of work done can help ensure the concepts remain understood.
- Computer programmes can reinforce mathematical concepts while making such activities fun. The websites in Chapter 12 are a useful source of information on such software.

How Teachers can Help

It is important that teachers understand how dyslexia can affect the progress of a student in Maths and that there are teaching strategies and techniques that have been successfully used in teaching Maths to students with dyslexia. Some of these include:

- Multi-sensory teaching so that the student will use concrete objects to establish abstract concepts;
- Ensuring the students understand the language and symbols used in Maths;

- Having appropriate aids available if the student has difficulty and ensuring the student knows how to use them;
- Use of computers to consolidate knowledge.

This is a huge area, as the difficulties the child has at age four are very different to those at age eight, age twelve or age sixteen. Therefore, outside the general principles above, the teaching strategies vary as the child develops.

There are many books and other aids that give specific advice to teachers at the different stages and these should be consulted when a teacher has difficulties teaching a particular child Maths. In the library section of the CD ROM *Understanding Dyslexia* there are lists of relevant books and some are listed below. The British Dyslexia Association (www.bda-dyslexia.org.uk) has fact sheets on Maths and dyslexia and on Maths resources.

Books for Teachers on Dyslexia and Maths

Chinn, S.J. and Ashcroft, J.R. (1998) *Mathematics for Dyslexics: A Teaching Handbook*, 2nd edn, London: Whurr.
Henderson, A. (2000) *Maths for the Dyslexic: A Practical Guide*, London: David Fulton.
Kay, J. and Yeo, D. (2003) *Dyslexia and Maths*, London: David Fulton.
Yeo, D. (2003) *Dyslexia, Dyspraxia and Mathematics*, London: Whurr.

12. Computers and Information Technology

This chapter will be of most use to parents and teachers. In it you will read about the following:

- How computers can help students with dyslexia;
- Keyboarding skills;
- Screening programmes;
- Assistive technology;
- Programmes that support learning;
- Sources of information;
- Irish suppliers.

Computers and information technology are of enormous help for all students. In particular, they provide essential and significant help to students with dyslexia. Such help is invaluable and this generation is very fortunate in having information and communications technology available to it.

How Computers can Help Students with Dyslexia

Computers can provide assistance in the following ways:

- Increased motivation, as computers may be fun to use;
- Programmes that adapt to proceed at the student's own pace so boredom and frustration do not set in. There can also be immediate feedback rather than waiting for the teacher's corrections;
- Assistive technology, where the computer may help students carry out tasks that they find difficult such as spelling, reading or writing;
- Programmes that help diagnose dyslexic characteristics;
- Word processors allow students to present work clearly and legibly. This can help achievement and self-esteem. It also helps students to complete work faster and allows for editing. Spelling and grammar checks are available;
- Programmes to help students gain literacy and numeracy skills. Students with dyslexia benefit from multi-sensory teaching and repetition, both of which computers provide;
- Programmes to help develop study skills or organisation skills;
- Speech recognition software so the student can dictate to the computer and obtain a typed copy;
- Access to websites on the topic of study skills or that provide study notes for subjects in the Leaving or Junior Certificate.

With so many programmes and products available, it is easy to become confused with the choice. Computer software is often expensive and comes packaged, so it is difficult to find out prior to purchase if a product is suitable. Ways of obtaining practical experience of the software include advice from teachers, demonstrations of software at conferences or exhibitions, or demonstration disks provided by suppliers or downloaded from the Internet. Students may use a particular software package in school or in a Dyslexia Association of Ireland workshop and find it of benefit. The websites listed at the end of this chapter also provide a means of obtaining current information.

VAT can be claimed back on the purchase of computers/assistive technology for home/personal use via Form VAT 61A.

Keyboarding Skills

At the present time, the main method of inputting information into the computer is keyboarding. To be able to use a word processor effectively, touch-typing skills or at least keyboard familiarity using eight fingers is needed. It takes the investment of time and effort to persevere to learn to touch-type but it is well worth the effort, particularly for the student with dyslexia who is likely to benefit so much from using word processors. It is very difficult for a person who uses the two-finger approach and looks at the keys to change over to touch-typing, so developing these skills as early as possible is recommended. Some students are well motivated and can learn by themselves. Others may need the discipline that comes from a course of structured learning with a teacher. Like all skills, keyboarding needs to be practised regularly if it is to develop and be maintained.

If the use of a word processor helps students to achieve, they should be able to produce homework, projects and house exams in this way. The reasonable accommodations allowed in state examinations include the use of a word processor for a small number of students. If the school is to assess whether a student would benefit from using a word processor in examinations, the student needs to be proficient in its use. This means that, in the case of a Junior Certificate student, good keyboarding skills should be in place by the end of second year.

The British Dyslexia Association's website has an information sheet on keyboard skills and touch-typing. It includes the criteria for choosing a touch-typing package for students with dyslexia and the names of recommended packages. One of the key recommendations is that the package should not use any 'near-words', for example 'hed', 'kik', as these could confuse the student with dyslexia who is trying to learn to spell correctly.

Screening Programmes

In 1996 the Computer Resource Centre at the University of Hull developed a diagnostic screening system called Cognitive Profiling System (CoPS) to be used in the four to six age group. It measured a child's reaction to various challenges on the computer screen. This has been developed into four programmes for different ages:

1. CoPS baseline for children between four years and five years and six months;
2. Lucid CoPS for children between four and eight years;
3. LASS Junior for individuals between eight and eleven years;
4. LASS Secondary for individuals between eleven and fifteen years.

All four programmes use standardised norms researched in the UK.

Assistive Technology

Assistive technology provides the student with help in doing tasks they find difficult. In the case of dyslexia, computer technology provides very real help for the student.

The main forms of assistive technology are:

- *Word processors with spelling and grammar checks.* These enable the student to provide written material of good quality. This is particularly useful if handwriting is poor and takes a lot of effort. It can be faster and easier than writing by hand provided the student has good keyboarding skills. It is also good for self-esteem to see one's work look well. Editing and rearranging text is easy, so students do not have to rewrite laboriously to produce a final copy. This facility also helps students who have sequencing difficulties, as it is easy to edit the text so as to rearrange the sequence of points. Mistakes are easy to correct as spelling and grammar checks are provided. Because the word processor minimises spelling and handwriting difficulties, students are free to concentrate on ideas and how they want to express them. It encourages them to be more adventurous and creative. It helps the student organise work as it can be saved and filed on the computer. *Alphasmart* is a machine that does word processing only. It can hold 64 pages of material in 8 separate files in its memory that can be downloaded to a printer or to a computer for filing. It has a small screen displaying four lines at a time. It is robust and relatively inexpensive.
- *Speech recognition software.* This allows the student dictate to the computer, which produces a typed copy on the screen. More

and more of these systems are coming on the market. The programmes need to learn the voice of the user so it takes time to train a system to an individual's voice. The user also needs training in being consistent in giving commands and punctuation instructions. Developing dictation accuracy is important for students with dyslexia, as they may have more difficulty identifying mistakes made on the screen and correcting them. *Dragon Naturally Speaking* is one such programme. Information sheets on speech recognition systems are available from BECTA, BDA and IANSYST websites which are listed at the end of this chapter.

- *Programmes that scan text and read it aloud. Kurzweil* is such a programme. It scans written material, displays it on-screen and reads it aloud. It can be used on texts suitable for young children all the way to college students. It is easy to see how such a system can benefit the student who is learning to read, but it is also of huge benefit to second- and third-level students who may have to read complicated text a number of times to extract the main points. By hearing as well as reading the text, this task can become much easier. The programme also displays and reads aloud Internet documents. It is possible to scan coloured documents although there is a cheaper. Version of Kurzweil that only uses black and white. Text sections can be highlighted in different colours and users can note or extract text to produce a study outline. Users are able to read along, take notes and highlight relevant text on-screen. Language tools such as a dictionary, thesaurus and phonetic spelling capability provide additional support. The student can add notes to the text, either written or by voice.
- *Read and Write* allows text to be read back and spoken as it is typed. Words can be highlighted as they are typed. There is a phonic spell checker that can speak the words aloud. There is a context-based word prediction facility. As the user types the first letter of a word, suggestions are made in the word prediction list. This reduces the number of keystrokes used, helping with speed and sentence construction.
- *Quickionary* Reading Pen. This hand-held reading pen can scan a word or line from any printed text, display the word(s) in large letters, read the word(s) aloud and define the word(s). It is possible to use a headset for private listening.
- *QuickLink* Pen is a 'Digital highlighter' for scanning information when away from the computer. It scans and stores the information and then downloads it to the PC. It is very useful for taking notes and quotes.

- *Electronic personal organisers* can include a diary, spreadsheet, database, word-processing facility, calculator, alarm and email facility. Some students with dyslexia can tend to be disorganised. Structuring their life with the use of such an organiser helps in recall of important facts and deadlines.
- *Textease* is a talking word processing package, with many of the facilities of desktop publishing. The speech options allow the user to listen to letters, words, sentences or all the text. In the multimedia version, video, animations and sound files can be added to pages.

Programmes that Support Learning

Examples of some of the software available are detailed below. Again the websites listed at the end of this chapter have comprehensive information on programmes.

- *Wordshark* combines the excitement of computer games with learning to spell and read. It offers 26 different games that use sound, graphics and text to teach and reinforce word recognition and spelling.
- *Starspell* helps develop spelling skills from the young child to teenagers. It uses the *look-cover-write-check* strategy. Every word is spoken and many have pictures. It is possible to create personal lists of words.
- *Numbershark* is a programme to help anyone improve basic numeracy. It uses a wide range of computer games to develop number skills. It offers 30 totally different games covering addition, subtraction, multiplication and division in ways that add meaning and understanding to these operations. It is suitable for ages six to adult.
- *Inspiration* is a programme to help students in structuring written work. People with dyslexia often prefer to think in pictures than in words. They like to use idea mapping – to build a visual map of ideas using pictures, colours, shapes and relationships. They use the technique for note-taking, remembering information and organising ideas for written work. *Inspiration* allows the student build pictures on screen and then convert the image to a linear outline. The outline can be copied into the word processor and used as a basis for writing.
- *Wordswork* is a multi-sensory programme on study skills. It was designed primarily for undergraduates with dyslexia but is very relevant for students at second level and for adults who want to

improve their skills before going back to formal education. It uses graphics, voice-overs, colour and humour to develop a variety of language skills that students with dyslexia (and others) need to address. Topics covered include essay writing, exam revision and time management.

Sources of Information

British Educational Communications and Technology
Agency (BECTA)
Website: www.becta.org.uk
Provides information sheets on:
• Special Needs and ICT;
• Dyslexia and ICT.

British Dyslexia Association (BDA)
Website: www.bda-dyslexia.org.uk
Provides information sheets on:
• Which computer and what will it cost;
• Keyboard skills and touch-typing;
• Literacy software;
• Maths software;
• Your computer talking to you;
• Talking to your computer (speech recognition software);
• Study support software.

IANSYST Ltd
The White House, Fen House, Fen Road Cambridge, CB4 1UN, UK.
Tel: 0044 1223 426644
Website: www.dyslexic.com

National Centre for Technology in Education
Dublin City University, Dublin 9.
Website: www.ncte.ie.
The booklet Special Educational Needs and Information and Communications Technology *provides information on:*
• ICT in Irish education;
• Department of Education and Science Grants;
• How to apply for grants;
• Use of the ICT in the classroom;
• Names of Irish suppliers;
• Web addresses of special needs discussion groups;
• Useful websites.

Irish Suppliers of ICT

Andrews Award Systems
38 Pine Valley Park, Dublin 16.
Tel: 01 4930011
Website: www.awardsys.net

Ash Technologies
Naas, Co. Kildare.
Tel: 045 882212
Website: www.ashtech.ie

Carroll Educational Supplies
Unit 5 Western Industrial Estate, Naas Road, Dublin 12.
Tel: 01 4567279

Computerspeak
Guinness Enterprise Centre, Taylor's Lane, Dublin 8.
Tel: 01 6777620
Website: www.computerspeak.ie

Diskovery Educational Software
Unit 2, Waveney, Howth Harbour, Co. Dublin.
Tel: 01 8063910
Website: www.diskovery.ie

Edtech Software Ltd
Murrisk, Westport, Co. Mayo.
Tel/Fax: 1850 923459
Website: www.edtech.ie

Jackson Technology
24 Kiltipper Ave, Aylesbury, Dublin 24.
Tel: 01 4518508 / 01 4624793
Website: www.jacksontechnology.com

13. Adults with Dyslexia

This chapter will be of most use to adults with dyslexia and to employers. In it you will read about:

- Dyslexia in adulthood;
- Psycho-educational assessment for adults;
- Dyslexia and how it affects adult life;
- Understanding dyslexia in the workplace;
- How employers can help;
- How adults with dyslexia can help themselves.

Dyslexia in Adulthood

A common misconception is that dyslexia, like measles or mumps, is a hazard of childhood. Sadly, this is not the case. And while it is acceptable, perhaps even amusing, when a child misreads a word or makes a basic spelling error, it is anything but funny when it happens to an adult. Dyslexia causes great embarrassment, anxiety and even humiliation to many adults who live in fear of being asked to read unfamiliar text aloud, to take detailed notes or to summarise the main points of a meeting.

Adults with dyslexia are found in all areas, from the board room to the box factory and from the operating theatre to the performance stage. Anyone, at any time of life or in any occupation, may have dyslexia. Those who work in an organisation employing twenty or more people are likely to have one or two colleagues with dyslexia. Some of these people may be qualified graduates working at very high levels. Dyslexia does not prevent high achievement provided the job suits the person. Many people with dyslexia find career success and fulfilment working for themselves or by choosing work areas that highlight their strengths and skills.

In an article in *Fortune Magazine* (May, 2002), Betsy Morris profiles some very successful business people – bankers, lawyers and entrepreneurs – all millionaires or billionaires, who succeeded in spite of major dyslexic difficulties. The best known on this side of the Atlantic is tycoon Richard Branson, who left school at sixteen and went on to build an aviation empire. Author Thomas G. West has written in detail about the achievements of engineers, scientists and information technology innovators who have dyslexia. In Harvard, he reports, dyslexia is known as the MIT (Massachusetts Institute of Technology) disease because so many of the students at this prestigious institute have the condition.

Sadly, for the majority of adults with dyslexia the story is not so positive. Many do not even know that they have a specific learning disability. They may have struggled for years to overcome difficulties whose origins they do not suspect. A common feature is fear: fear of being found out, fear they will not be able to cope with the next challenge, fear that someone will discover the strategies they use to cover up or fear that they may just be stupid and ineffective.

We have already seen that dyslexia is not merely a difficulty with literacy and language learning. It affects all aspects of information processing, short- and long-term memory and organisational skills. It may also affect mathematical processing and physical co-ordination. Going hand-in-hand with these difficulties, and often more damaging, is the lack of confidence and self-esteem caused by years of academic struggle or failure.

How is dyslexia identified in an adult man or woman? How is it seen beneath the layers of strategies and coping mechanisms that have been developed by resourceful and inventive people to hide what they consider to be their own inadequacies? The list of indicators for adults is included in Chapter 2.

Remember that despite the difficulties an individual with dyslexia may have, there can be strengths, including:

- Having a skill at visualising, i.e. thinking in pictures;
- Having good practical, problem-solving abilities;
- Being creative and innovative;
- Having the ability to think 'outside the box';
- Having good spatial ability;
- Possibly having excellent computer skills;
- Being patient and determined in spite of difficulties.

The checklist in Chapter 2 is not comprehensive. Many people experience some of the difficulties listed and may also have some of the skills listed above. However, if the difficulties are numerous and they are causing a problem in the person's life, then further investigation would be wise. Perhaps, the strongest indicator of a dyslexic-type difficulty is a deep-seated feeling in the individual that something is amiss. Many adults, when diagnosed with dyslexia, reported that they always knew they were somehow different but they did not know why. Many believed, as one woman put it, that they had a *lazy brain* or that they were simply not very smart.

The Psycho-Educational Assessment for Adults

The only way in which dyslexia can be positively identified in an adult is by carrying out a thorough psycho-educational assessent.There are four stages in the identification of dyslexia according to McLoughlin, Fitzgibbon and Young (1994):

1. Information gathering;
2. Psychological testing and diagnosis;
3. Developing an understanding of dyslexia;
4. Taking action.

Information gathering

This can be more difficult than one would imagine. Obviously it is necessary to have information on a condition in order to detect its existence. So many adults who have dyslexia have never even heard the word and have no idea how it affects learning. They are, therefore, unlikely to seek assessment unless encouraged by someone who knows about the condition. Anecdotal evidence records that parents are often identified following psychological assessment of their children. They find that the difficulties experienced by their children are so similar to their own that they are prompted to explore the possibility that they, too, are affected.

Psychological testing and diagnosis

The second step, psychological testing, is a more contentious issue. It is costly, difficult to access and not everyone believes that it is essential. Psycho-educational assessment is carried out by a psychologist and can range in cost from €350 to €500. There is no state provision for adults, even for those who are unemployed or who have a medical card. It can also be hard to locate a suitably qualified psychologist and waiting lists tend to be long. The Dyslexia Association of Ireland funds adults who would otherwise be unable to access assessment. This facility depends on funding from the Department of Education and Science, which is not guaranteed. A list of psychologists in private practice can be found on the website of the Psychological Society of Ireland (www.psihq.ie).

Is assessment necessary?

It is important to discover just why a learning difficulty exists because unless you know the precise nature of the problem, it is not going to be possible to deal with it effectively. Psycho-educational assessments for adults are about pinpointing the difficulty and advising on remediation. It is not about putting a label on the person. A diagnosis of lung cancer does not create a stigmatising label. Instead it gives medical experts the information they need to prescribe suitable treatment. Likewise, a diagnosis of dyslexia enables a person to begin the process of dealing with the condition.

It is often an enormous relief for adults who have felt stupid and inadequate all through life to realise that they have an identifiable difficulty. Adults with dyslexia are entitled to this knowledge about themselves. Knowledge empowers and knowing about a condition is the first step towards managing it.

The argument is sometimes made that, as some adults have been upset by their psycho-educational assessment, the procedure is unhelpful. This is not logical. The problem was not with the assessment in itself. Appropriate assessment with a competent and sensitive professional is a very therapeutic experience. The cognitive testing that is carried out by a psychologist, the personal observation and the dialogue between client and professional all are central to the whole assessment process.

The technology now exists to carry out screening and certain assessment procedures on computer. Screening tests, whether paper or computer based, can be a valuable starting point but they do not provide comprehensive information and a basis for future action. Computer-based assessments, however sophisticated, lack the human element. There are many issues for the newly diagnosed adult to deal with, such as regret for wasted years, anger at past treatment in school or at work, or fear of the future. These are best handled professionally by a trained psychologist.

Only a psychologist may carry out the necessary psychometric testing.

> The accurate diagnosis of dyslexia requires the measurement of general ability and working memory. Any procedure that fails to incorporate appropriate cognitive tests is likely to produce both false positives (i.e. the incorrect identification of a person who has low intelligence as dyslexic) and false negatives (the failure to identify a dyslexic person as such because they have developed strategies to compensate for their dyslexia).
> (McLoughlin, Fitzgibbon, Young, 1994: 29)

The authors add that the appropriate assessment of intelligence is one of the most crucial factors in diagnosis. This stands to reason: there are many reasons why adults have literacy difficulties and dyslexia is only one of them. While the effects of literacy difficulties are similar, the causes are very different. The results of the International Adult Literacy Survey published in 1997 indicated that 25 per cent of Irish adults had pronounced literacy problems. The reasons for these difficulties could be early school leaving, irregular school attendance, overcrowded classrooms, lack of family support for learning, low academic ability or dyslexia. If the latter two factors are confused, as they often were in the schoolrooms of the past, the result can be disastrous.

The assessment process

The purpose of a psycho-educational assessment for adults is to determine whether they have a dyslexic-type difficulty, the nature and extent of the problem and how the person can be helped to cope. The focus of the assessment therefore is on finding out how these adults learn and in helping them to use their best learning channels. Its aim is positive – to put the person in the driving seat in relation to their own lives – but the process can be daunting.

The psycho-educational assessment begins with a review of the person's family and school history. Areas of difficulty encountered are listed and family incidence of dyslexia is noted. Cognitive assessment is carried out using appropriate tests. The tester is interested in how the person tackles different items in the test and in the relative strengths they show. Reading, writing and spelling skills are also looked at, with a view to identifying problem areas and suggesting strategies to overcome difficulties. The procedure may last from two to three hours and will probably include discussion on the results of the assessment and advice on future action.

The most positive result of a psycho-educational assessment for an adult is often the validation that it provides. Self-esteem and self-confidence are likely to be very badly affected by adverse school experiences and failure to reach potential in the workplace. A positive assessment often provides the encouragement necessary to go for job promotion or to take on further study. Knowing about dyslexia and the support that now exists at third level can be the key to a new future.

Practical help for adults with severe literacy difficulties

Many adults who opt for psycho-educational assessment do so because of frustration with reading and spelling difficulties that continue to cause distress. If the assessment reveals dyslexia, then they will want some practical help with literacy. Ideally, an adult with dyslexia should work with a specifically trained teacher who utilises the information provided by a thorough psycho-educational assessment to devise an effective teaching programme. As quoted in the

Moser Report, research found that 'between 550 and 600 hours of instruction are needed to become fully literate and numerate'. While this level of tuition may not be possible outside of a full-time course, best results are obtained when teaching is provided on an intensive and consistent basis. Tutoring adults with dyslexia successfully requires considerable skill and training. The Dyslexia Association of Ireland maintains a list of such teachers and this is available to members. The association also sponsors a full-time course for adults. Tuition may also be obtained through the adult literacy services, which now have some tutors experienced in working with adults with dyslexia. Information can be obtained from the National Adult Literacy Agency, or from local Vocational Education Committees.

Dyslexia and How it Affects Adult Life

Once a positive diagnosis has been reached, the adult with dyslexia must then begin to gain an understanding of the condition in order to come to terms with it. Dyslexia affects all aspects of people's lives, not just their school years. When a person learns differently and takes longer to develop skills to an automatic level, this has an impact on a wide variety of areas such as learning to drive a car, using a computer, acquiring a second language, handling tax affairs or securing a house mortgage. All of these everyday tasks can be complicated by the information-processing styles of a person with dyslexia.

To what degree dyslexia affects a person's life depends on many factors: the age at which the condition was diagnosed, the degree of severity, the ability of the individual, the type and quality of support received – both educational and social – and even the personality of the individual. Some people are lucky enough to have had their dyslexia identified as children and to have received support through their school years. They have had an opportunity to understand their own learning difficulties and to take them into account when planning further education or choosing a career. The fact that they have overcome basic literacy difficulties and even secured satisfactory results in examinations does not mean that they have been 'cured' of their dyslexia. Information processing difficulties, poor short-term memory, auditory processing deficits or hand–eye co-ordination difficulties do not go away. A person who chose a work area where literacy was not of vital importance could find that promotion or changing work practices require them to read and write a great deal more. Another could discover that dealing with clients abroad demands second language skills that were not acquired at school. Updating computer skills, learning to use new technology or new equipment, re-training that has to be undertaken in certain sectors of industry can all be difficult for a person who thought that dyslexia was left behind with school days. If the difficulties encountered at school were severe, then the adult may well have a reluctance to re-enter a learning situation.

Adults, particularly young adults who have recently completed their education, may find that the working environment is not as supportive of people with dyslexia as third-level institutions. A great deal of help and support is now provided at third level and it is very acceptable to declare one's dyslexia. In the working world the situation is very different. A major dilemma facing young people about to enter the workforce is whether to inform prospective employers that they have dyslexia. Despite the passing of the Employment Equality Act in 1998 and the Equal Status Act in 2000, the position of workers with dyslexia is still not clear. If a person is dismissed or not hired because of dyslexia then there may be a case for the employer to answer. But it is most unlikely that any employer is going to lay themselves open to such question. However, if a job candidate declares on an application form or at interview that they have dyslexia, even if they also have impressive qualifications, will they get the job? If they do not get the job, they will never know whether stating their dyslexia had anything to do with it.

Adults who reach the age of 40 or 50 before being identified as dyslexic often experience great anger and frustration because of their learning difficulties. This can make them uncomfortable people to live or work with and can have implications for personal and family relationships. The tensions and stresses caused by trying to cover up learning difficulties or to cope in a world that thinks and functions differently to oneself may cause people with dyslexia to seek release in alcohol or other addictive behaviours. In *Dyslexia and Counselling* Rosemary Scott says:

> I have certainly encountered a remarkable degree of alcohol and drug-related anxiety conditions in both dyslexic men and women. In this respect, I would estimate that, as a group, they are significantly more likely to use drink and drugs to cope with their anxiety than non-dyslexics are.
> (Scott, 2004: 169)

Much publicity is given to famous people with dyslexia, such as Albert Einstein, W.B. Yeats, Richard Branson and others, but less attention is paid to those who fail to cope. Adults who dropped out of school or under-achieved because of dyslexia are more likely to find themselves in low-paying jobs or unemployed. This, in turn, affects the life chances of their children as the link between literacy difficulties and poverty is well established.

In extreme cases, young men (and it is almost invariably young men) get into trouble with the law and end up in prison. A British study reported that the young offenders surveyed first got into trouble while 'mitching' from school. They skipped school because learning was unrewarding and they had been left behind by the age of ten.

Understanding Dyslexia in the Workplace

The consequences of having dyslexia depend very much on the time and the culture. When literacy was neither vital to daily life nor very valued, having dyslexia was not a problem. In the future, it may well be that developments in information technology will make literacy, as we know it, irrelevant: reading and writing may be as outdated as the horse and cart. In this scenario, the person with dyslexia would not be at a disadvantage at all. Possibly, with good creative, visual and problem-solving skills, they would have a distinct advantage. However, in today's society, those with dyslexia are in an unenviable position. Not only is work, travel and leisure dominated by the written word, but skill in planning, organisation and time management are more important than ever before. Completing tasks to a time schedule, absorbing new information quickly and working under pressure are requirements of every workplace. None of these come easily to the person with dyslexia.

Organisation and time management

If one word were applied to the adult with dyslexia who is having problems in the workplace, it would probably be *disorganised*. Where the words 'could try harder' are often used in school reports, the adult equivalent very often is 'can't get their act together'. Planning and organising, setting out timetables, distinguishing between the important and the urgent, remembering appointments, passing on telephone messages and meeting deadlines can be exceptionally difficult for many people with dyslexia. Many complain of a tendency to get bogged down, overwhelmed by the workload and very stressed.

Initial job training

The initial training may be insufficient, in that a dyslexic person may not have the same learning style as other employees. Skilled and well-qualified workers have reported an absence of flexibility in the approach to training in many firms. Research has indicated that it can take a person with dyslexia longer to acquire a skill to an automatic level. Once the skill is acquired, performance may be similar or better than average, but in pressured work situations this extra time may not be given. Awareness of the skills as well as the difficulties of people with dyslexia would help greatly in this area.

Information processing

So many office workers today suffer from information overload that the pressure on people with dyslexia can be almost unbearable. Most adults with dyslexia who work in professional or white-collar jobs have good reading skills. They may read quite fluently and have excellent comprehension but their reading speed may be slower. They may also need to exercise more care not to misread a word or phrase. Letters, emails, reports, journals, magazine articles, newspaper reports – the amount of reading required to keep abreast of developments is a major burden and the time it takes often eats into leisure and family time.

Similarly, when it comes to letter or report writing, editing, checking spelling and grammar, double checking figures for reversals and placement errors, managing appointments diaries and recording telephone messages, extra time is also needed. Many people with dyslexia have problems with clerical speed and accuracy, so care is essential. While the advent of the word processor has made life easier, it has also meant that very few people now have personal secretaries. Most people must produce their own written work. It is no longer sufficient to be a good engineer, one must also be able to write a clear and properly spelt report and perform tasks at high speed. A worker at a call centre must be able not only to do the job but also must complete each task within a stated time and meet hourly targets of calls answered.

Positive aspects of dyslexia in the workplace

It may sometimes sound as if adults with dyslexia experience nothing but difficulties. This is certainly not the case. While certain administrative tasks may take a person with dyslexia longer to complete, there are many areas where specific skills more than compensate. Many people with dyslexia have made successful careers in medicine, business, architecture, engineering and, of course, in the creative arts as writers, actors, artists and sculptors.

One of the compensatory aspects of having a different learning style is that it often enables very fresh and innovative thinking, an ability to see solutions where others see problems and the diligence and perseverance to put these into effect. Learning to cope with a school system that does not understand you, overcoming obstacles, keeping going in spite of failures and having to work harder than others to achieve the same results or less, build up strength and a determination that is worth having in any work situation. Scott (2004) cites four authorities to back up her claim that 'dyslexic people do work much harder than others and are more persistent'. Employers who are too narrowly focused on accredited qualifications, or whose work practices allow for no variation, may miss out badly on possible employees. An example is the man who set up and successfully ran a company while on a training scheme. When the company became viable and the job was advertised, his application was rejected because he had no formal qualifications. If neat handwriting and good spelling is the criteria, neither Albert Einstein nor W.B. Yeats would get past the Human Resources desk, Richard Branson would not make it to interview stage and Steve Redgrave (five Olympic gold medals to his credit) might not even complete the application form.

Employer awareness

In 1999, the Dyslexia Association of Ireland carried out a small survey of 100 Irish companies in the private sector. While the majority of firms that responded claimed that they would be willing to employ a person with dyslexia, only 7 per cent of the respondents actually knew that they had someone with dyslexia on their staff. Given that many of these companies employed more than ten people and some employed more than one hundred, it is inconceivable that the number known to have dyslexia is so small. The lack of knowledge of dyslexia displayed by some employers was striking.

One respondent said their firm would not hire someone with dyslexia because the nature of their business required all employees 'to be of at least average ability'.

Dyslexia is a hidden disability. When a person attends for interview in a wheelchair or with a guide dog, it is quite obvious that this person has a disability. If an employer hires such a person, they do so in full knowledge of the disability. Dyslexia is an unknown entity to many employers. The assumption is often made that if a person has dyslexia, they cannot read at all. Regrettably many people still assume that dyslexia means illiteracy or possibly impaired mental functioning. Things have not changed so much since Albert Einstein lost two lecturing posts because of his erratic spelling and poor handwriting.

Equality legislation in Ireland prohibits discrimination against people with disabilities but proving that someone has been discriminated against in employment is extremely difficult. Anecdotal evidence suggests that it is happening and that employees are being bullied because of dyslexia but the facts are hard to establish. It would be a great pity if employers did not take full advantage of the particular skills that people with dyslexia have to offer. The creativity and problem solving skills, the ability to think differently and devise coping strategies are all talents that need to be fostered in the working environment. Diversity needs to be cherished. If working practices demand only square pegs for square holes, what happens when a round hole appears?

How Employers can Help

Employers are in an enormously powerful situation in relation to workers with dyslexia. They can determine whether the person becomes a productive and happy member of staff or whether their employee becomes a nervous, stressed-out wreck who contributes little to the organisation or to their own well-being. Some relatively simple procedures would make life easier and work more productive, not only for employees with dyslexia, but perhaps for all staff.

- Become aware of dyslexia. It is a fact of working life. Perhaps 6 to 8 per cent of the workforce are affected by dyslexia to some extent. A literacy difficulty may explain why some workers are reluctant to keep records, write reports or even seek promotion. It may also explain difficulties with time management and reactions to perceived authority figures. Many adults with dyslexia who have unhappy memories of school days carry the fear and resentment felt as children to their work situation.

- Create an open environment in which employees have no fear that declaring a difficulty will result in dismissal or sidelining. Trade unions can be helpful here in setting up mechanisms to manage access to information and support. If a dyslexic problem is identified, it can be taken into account. A difficulty that is being covered up is much more likely to result in mistakes than one that is recognised. Colleagues can be encouraged to help each other out. The good reader may proofread written work in return for help with a technical matter. Work can be allocated to suit the talents of the individual and thus the employer gets the best from every worker.

- Look at the whole person. Reading may not be a strength but there may be many other skills and abilities that are untapped. Many people with dyslexia have great interpersonal skills and are very vocal; others have exceptional facility with information technology. Adults with dyslexia have usually learned patience and tolerance and so make understanding trainers and instructors.

- Remember that staff with high-level qualifications can still have dyslexia and that it may affect their work, particularly if they are trying to cover up the condition.

- Use the many support systems that exist. Outside specialists can provide screening and psycho-educational assessment if necessary. Individual tuition and support for employees is available and studies in the UK have found that productivity increases when areas of difficulty are targeted.

- Consider how technology can help. Word processing packages with spell and grammar checks can work wonders. Voice-operated software, screen readers, scanners, mobile phones with recording memory, electronic dictionaries, talking calculators, reading pens and electronic organisers – one or more of these may solve the problem (see Chapter 12 for full details).

- Consider low-tech solutions. People with dyslexia often find that increasing print size to I4 points, using a plain font or changing the background colour on a computer makes a huge improvement in legibility. Photocopying information on coloured paper, use of colour coding, coloured hi-lighters and coloured transparent sheets to cover reading material may also help. Instructions do not always have to be given in densely printed form. Short, clear sentences in plain English and well spaced on the paper are more accessible for all workers. A picture is worth a thousand words to a person with dyslexia. Illustrations, diagrams, flow charts and mindmaps can be enormously helpful. Visual literacy is a skill not to be underestimated. Some day we may all need to have it!

- Be flexible. A key factor in dyslexia is difference. Employers can view this difference as a positive or a negative. If a worker with dyslexia does not find a particular system or training practice suits their learning style, ask them what would suit. There may be another way and it may even be better.

How Adults with Dyslexia can Help Themselves

Adults with dyslexia must remember that they are a minority of the population. While minorities have rights, they must adapt to living in a world that does not see things the same way as they do. For the person with dyslexia, the question of how they adapt to their condition is crucial. Ultimately, success will depend on the action they take to manage their own lives and reach their own potential.

Adults whose dyslexia was identified in childhood are relatively lucky. At best, they may have had remedial support and been enabled to make a smooth transition from school to third level and on to the workplace. At worst, they knew the reason for any learning difficulties they encountered. The following points are directed to those identified in adulthood and also to those who feel they have not fully come to terms with their dyslexia:

- Find out as much as possible about your particular situation. Dyslexia can be mild or severe. It can affect the academically gifted, the average learner or the less able. It can be accompanied by attention and concentration problems, dyspraxia, speech and language processing difficulties and anxiety conditions. It is very important to be aware of your profile. The person who can tell you this is the psychologist who carries out the psycho-educational assessment. Do not be afraid to ask – it is your life. If you were assessed as a child and did not receive this information then consider having a new assessment and asking questions.
- Learn about dyslexia. There are numerous sources of information from books and websites to talks and conferences. The more you understand about the condition, the more you will understand yourself. You will also learn that it is a two-edged sword – it carries advantages as well as disadvantages. Learn

to capitalise on your strengths. Concentrate on what you can do rather than on what you cannot.

- Take positive action. If you were advised by the assessing psychologist to seek professional help to improve your literacy or support you in further study, then go ahead. The Dyslexia Association of Ireland maintains a list of qualified teachers who offer individual tuition to adults with dyslexia. The Dyslexia Association also sponsors a full-time course for adults, which is administered by FAS. This course is a very useful means for adults who have been unemployed or working in the home to upgrade their literacy skills and acquire computer training.

- If you left school without achieving formal qualifications, consider the possibility of going back into education. There is a wide variety of choices – from night classes at your local college of further education to access courses for university. As an adult, with life experience and maturity, you may be surprised at your success.

- The National Adult Literacy Agency now offers support to adults whose literacy difficulties are caused by dyslexia. *Keys for Learning,* a document published by NALA, provides information on services available. NALA can be contacted at 76 Lower Gardiner Street, Dublin 1, Tel: 01 8554332, Email: literacy@nala.ie, Website: www.nala.ie. Information can also be obtained from local Vocational Educational Committees.

- The Adult Education Guidance Initiative offers information, advice and guidance on a one-to-one basis for adults who wish to return to education. This valuable service is provided by the Department of Education and Science and can be accessed through the National Centre for Guidance in Education, 42–43 Prussia Street, Dublin 7, Tel: 01 8690715, Email: info@ncge.ie, Website: www.ncge.ie.

- Third-level colleges, institutes of technology, colleges of further education and training centres are all now more aware of dyslexia and some excellent support services are in place. Many provide specialist tuition, facilitate note-taking in class and allow extra time or use of technology in exams.

- Employers are increasingly becoming aware of dyslexia. There is still a lot of improvement needed in this area but if you have an understanding employer you may be able to make adjustments in your work situation to minimise your particular difficulties and improve your own productivity.

- You may find that the attitude of family and friends towards you changes when it is discovered that you are a capable person with dyslexia who has been hampered by the difficulty. You may also find that your self-esteem rises and you become more confident. This is perhaps the most common side effect of receiving a diagnosis of dyslexia. When your confidence reaches the level of being able to say, 'I have dyslexia, so what?' then you have made a major leap forward.

- Investigate what modern technology can offer. Third-level students may be eligible for grants for computers and software. Employers may be willing to supply equipment if the benefits can be demonstrated. Explore the possibility of getting VAT back on equipment that is deemed necessary by a psychologist.
- Be aware that not all of your difficulties may be the result of dyslexia. There are other hidden learning difficulties such as attention deficit hyperactivity disorder and dyspraxia. Like dyslexia, these are life-long conditions and so may affect adults. It may be necessary to consult professionals in these areas also, to get your life under control. Some people, particularly those whose learning difficulties caused distress in childhood, may find that they need professional counselling before beginning to tackle the practical task of getting help with reading and writing. You need a clear head and no other side-issues that might hamper learning.
- Finally, your own attitude towards your dyslexia will be the most significant factor. If you believe that fate has treated you unfairly and that the world owes you a living, you are going to compound your problems. If, on the other hand, you decide that dyslexia is not going to prevent you from achieving your goals and you are prepared to put in the hard work and use every strategy you know to get round, through and over the obstacles in your path, you will get there, as many others have before you.

14. Non-Teaching Interventions

In this chapter you will read about various alternative approaches that are proposed as ways of remediating the deficits in processing now generally acknowledged as being part of dyslexia. These are usually interventions other than teaching methods:

- Interventions based on neuro-developmental delay;
- Vision therapies;
- Auditory therapies;
- Nutrition and diet;
- Combined teaching/other therapies.

In Chapter 2 the theoretical explanations for dyslexia were examined. Research studies continue in a range of areas such as speed of processing, phonological awareness, visual processing, balance and automaticity. The main causal theories may prove to complement one another. They offer explanation of dyslexia at different levels of processing.

Each of these theories has led to the development of practical programmes of intervention. Many of these address aspects of functioning other than the activity of reading and writing. They may be considered as *non-teaching* interventions to differentiate them from the traditional process of learning to read and write in school. They do not replace it. Most claim that, by providing additional stimulus and a systematic programme that develops an aspect of the child's functioning, their therapy also results in improved literacy skills. The level of scientific research upon which they base their claims is a crucial factor in evaluating the possible efficacy of any one particular programme. Dyslexia is a complex syndrome. People with dyslexia will have a range of difficulties along a continuum of degree of difficulty. The particular programme may have very beneficial results for the child in improving, perhaps, visual perception or motor skills. What is not clear is the link with dyslexia. When these skills improve, they may well contribute to a greater reading readiness for a host of reasons. It is important to remember that there is no *cure* for developmental dyslexia. Since it is not a disease, methods of intervention may improve functioning if the scientific evidence is there to prove it.

Reading is a secondary, not a primary skill. This means it is a taught skill for all people and thus, while non-teaching interventions can help some children who have deficits in particular areas of processing, they will still continue to need great support and informed teaching methods to allow them to become expert readers and writers.

There are a number of types of interventions, each emanating from a particular theoretical viewpoint, *not all of which have been proven by sound scientific research.*

Interventions Based on Neuro-Developmental Delay

Many children with developmental dyslexia are clumsy and have difficulty with co-ordination and, in particular, with fine motor control. Several therapies have emerged in recent years that claim that specific learning difficulties are related to delay in attaining developmental milestones and omission of developmental steps such as crawling and poor sensory-motor development. One group of interventions is based on the theory that certain primary reflexes may not have been inhibited as the child developed, resulting in a variety of difficulties, many of which are observed in children with dyslexia. The hard evidence of the relationship between such neuro-developmental delay and dyslexia is not yet available. However, there is serious ongoing research taking place. At the time of going to press, a group of research students in TCD are engaged in examining the retained primary reflexes theory.

As one would expect, interventions based on these theories focus on remediating fluency of movement, blocking primary reflexes, integrating sensory co-ordination and improving balance. There are a number of such therapies available in Ireland and Britain. There is no doubt that many children benefit from such programmes, as other children benefit from, say, speech and language development programmes or counselling. What has to be asked when considering the benefits of such therapies is how scientifically accurate are the theories of the brain and of the *dyslexic* brain upon which the programme is built. How much does it take into account known facts about how the printed word is processed? Until there is greater scientific evidence, it is wise to be cautious.

Vision Therapies

There are a significant number of persons with dyslexia whose primary difficulty lies in the visual processing of print. When developmental dyslexia was first being researched, Orton called it *strephosymbolia*, a mixing up of symbols. The classic caricature of how a person with dyslexia writes is with inversions and reversals of letters. This characterisation of dyslexia focused on the visual aspects of processing. Later researchers have categorised dyslexia as *deep* when phonological difficulties are particularly pronounced and as *surface* or *eidetic* when visual processing difficulties are to the fore. Some therapies specifically address visual processing difficulties. There is no doubt that some people with dyslexia experience difficulty maintaining smooth eye movement across the page and moving from line to line. Poor visual memory for letter patterns is not uncommon. Some people experience light sensitivity and respond better to background colour other than white, and print colour other than black. A significant number have difficulty with visual perception, which may suggest the presence of co-existing dyspraxia.

Helen Irlen developed a method of testing for what was called *scotopic sensitivity*, later known as Irlen Syndrome and now called visual stress. Subsequent studies have identified visual differences that can be alleviated by the use of coloured lenses or acetate overlays. Visual stress is not unique to persons with dyslexia

There are many unanswered questions around the area of visual processing and there is much ongoing research attempting to address them. One member of the Dyslexia Research Group in Trinity College is involved in such research. John Stein's magnocellular theory, which implicates visual processing, is currently one of the most influential of the causal theories of dyslexia. As with the movement and balance programmes, practitioners who subscribe to a visual causal theory report improvement in reading efficiency.

Auditory Therapies

The third category of interventions addresses the auditory and phonological deficits that are seen as core indicators of *deep* dyslexia. These include programmes aimed at auditory stimulation through music and structured listening techniques. There is a need for more scientific research to validate their claims.

Nutrition and Diet

A fourth category of *alternative therapies* uses the information derived from research into the relationship between diet and brain functioning. There is a body of research that has been examining the role of essential fatty acids (EFAs) and highly unsaturated fatty acids (HUFAs) in brain function. There appears to be a higher than average level of deficiency of essential fatty acids (omega three) among many people who are dyslexic, dyspraxic and have attention deficit disorder. Dr Alex Richardson (Oxford) has presented very thorough research findings on the beneficial effects of taking fish oil supplements. It should be pointed out, however, that one does not necessarily need to take supplements. A balanced diet, rich in natural sources of omega oils such as oily fish (salmon, tuna and mackerel) and vegetable oils and seeds (sunflower, flax/linseed, pumpkin and sesame) may be all that is needed.

Combined Teaching/Other Therapies

Some interventions combine theory-based therapy with teaching. These include techniques to develop speed-reading and the ability to visualise. Because of the complexity of dyslexia, and the uniqueness of learning strengths and weaknesses among people with dyslexia, some will benefit from these activities. Others will not. The most effective teaching methods for people with dyslexia are those which are multi-sensory, follow a structured, step-by-step programme, and are built on a principle of over-learning.

Conclusion

Because dyslexia affects a cluster of abilities and because each person's dyslexia is so individual, it is likely that any one of these therapies may address a particular area on your child's profile. Alternative therapies can be very expensive and the one you select may not produce the desired effect. In many cases good nutrition, good exercise and physical education programmes, more explicit listening exercises at home and the ordinary helps, tailored a little more individually to your child, may be just as beneficial. However, if you wish to explore an alternative route ask these relevant questions:

- Is there solid scientific evidence that this method is effective?
- What is the known link between the theory and dyslexia?
- Does this intervention claim to cure dyslexia?
- Is there evidence that the effects of the intervention persist into the long term and are not simple short-term improvements that disappear when the intervention stops?

As has been said, there are solid scientific studies currently in train around a number of these alternative therapies. The current state of play was well expressed by Rod Nicholson, when summing up the proceedings of the 2004 BDA International Conference on Dyslexia:

> There is growing (but still disputed) evidence that at least some dyslexic children benefit from non-reading support aimed at eliminating problems that make it especially hard for them to learn to read. These complementary approaches include dietary improvements, use of tinted lenses, elimination of primitive reflexes and use of exercise treatments ... one can see them as trying to equip the climbers (children with dyslexia) with better footgear so that, whichever path they're on, they will climb more easily and more safely.

15. Frequently Asked Questions

In this chapter you will find some very brief answers to common questions. This chapter may also be used as a quick reference. More detailed information on all topics is provided in the foregoing chapters.

What is Dyslexia?

This simple question is one of the hardest to answer. Coming from the Greek words *dys/dus* meaning *bad* or *hard* and *lexis* meaning *language*, dyslexia is, literally, a difficulty with language, specifically written language. It makes it hard for people to read, write and spell correctly. It is a genetic condition, not related to overall intelligence and not caused by laziness on the part of the individual. It occurs in 6 to 8 per cent of the population.

What is the Difference between Dyslexia and Specific Learning Disability?

Specific learning disability (SLD) is an umbrella term for a number of learning difficulties including dyslexia. While dyslexia is often used as a synonym for SLD, there are other conditions that are also classed as specific learning disabilities – ADD/ADHD, Dyspraxia and Asperger's Syndrome are probably the most common. A person with dyslexia may well have one or more of these conditions also.

Why does my Child have Dyslexia?

Dyslexia is a genetic condition, so it is very likely that your child inherited it from a parent or grandparent. There is no way that a parent or teacher can cause a child to have dyslexia and there is no way to prevent it. There is no reason for any parent to feel guilty about a child's dyslexia or to be ashamed of the condition.

Why does my Child have to be Assessed?

In order to deal with any problem it is necessary to have a great deal of information about it. Dyslexia can be mild, moderate or severe. The child affected may be very bright, of average ability or of less than average academic ability. This information can only be gleaned from the results of tests administered by a qualified psychologist. Learning difficulties may result in behaviour problems, which may be seen as the cause, not the result, of the difficulty. A child with dyslexia may also have attention deficits or speech and language difficulties. The diagnosis and remediation of a specific

learning difficulty is a complex process, so assessment by an educational specialist is necessary if a comprehensive education plan
is to be put into effect.

How can I get an Assessment?

A school may request psycho-educational assessment through the
National Educational Psychological Service. This service is free but
it can take a long time for such an assessment to be obtained, as
there is limited access to the service and schools must prioritise the
students with the greatest need. Many parents, therefore, are
forced to seek private assessments. Such assessments may be
obtained privately from the Dyslexia Association of Ireland or from
psychologists in private practice. The Psychological Society of Ireland (www.psihq.ie) maintains a list of qualified psychologists.
Assessments cost from €350 to €500 in 2005 and may take several
weeks or months to arrange.

Will my Child be Labelled?

The word *label* is the issue here. Identifying a problem, making a
diagnosis and giving a name to a condition – all of these are necessary parts of dealing with dyslexia. Making sure that a diagnosis
of dyslexia is not used as an excuse by a child for not trying to learn
or as a stigmatising label by an uninformed person is a matter for
the parent.

How Often do I Need to have my Child Assessed?

In general, a full reassessment should be necessary only at critical points in the child's academic career. It may be advisable
before transferring from primary to secondary school, particularly
if the first assessment was carried out when the child was in first
or second class. A full assessment should not be carried out
within a year of the original. A recent assessment (one less than
two years old) is very helpful when applying for reasonable
accommodations in the Leaving Certificate or for accessing
disability services at third level. Other than on these occasions a
full assessment should only be considered in the light of individual cases.

Do Children Grow out of Dyslexia?

No. Dyslexia is a life-long condition. Though a child may learn to read, write and spell adequately, the underlying difficulty will always be present. It may cause difficulties in learning a foreign language, in learning to drive a car or in acquiring other skills.

Do Children with Dyslexia ever Learn to Read?

The majority of people with dyslexia do learn to read if given the appropriate help, particularly if this help is received at an early age. Becoming a confident speller is rather more difficult and some people experience this problem all through their lives. However, these problems can now be overcome to a large extent through the use of information technology.

Will my Child have to go to a Special School?

Only children who have a severe reading delay, as indicated by the fact they are performing at or below the 2nd percentile, are entitled to attend special reading schools. There are three reading schools in Dublin, one in Cork and a number of special reading units in national schools around the country. These cater for a relatively small number of children, who attend for a maximum of two years. The majority of children with dyslexia attend regular schools.

What Kind of Secondary School Should I Choose?

The choice of school is a very personal thing and the individual needs of the child must be taken into account. While there is no ideal school for children with dyslexia, a dyslexia-friendly school may be identified by policy on admission and participation by students with disabilities (see Chapter 8).

Can I do Home Schooling?

In theory you can, but few parents feel equal to this challenge. Advocates of home schooling argue that it allows children to work at their own pace and learn in their own individual style. Critics of the system say that children need the company of peers and that the social, sporting and cultural aspects of school are just as important as the learning.

Will my Child be Able to go to College?

This depends on the overall academic ability of the child, the severity of the dyslexia and the amount of help the child receives. Statistics from the third-level sector in Ireland record ever-increasing numbers of students with dyslexia and colleges now offer great support. When completing CAO forms, it is important for students with dyslexia to tick the box that allows access to the Disability Support Service at third level. It is also important to note that education has become much more flexible and students can progress from PLC to Higher Certificate and to degree-level courses (see Chapter 8).

How can I Teach my Child at Home?

Teaching and parenting are both highly important and demanding occupations. While many teachers are also parents, the roles are not similar. Teachers are trained to be objective and unemotional. Few parents can remain uninvolved when trying to teach a child with a learning difficulty. In general, the teaching done by parents is best done informally and by providing support as requested by the child. Formal teaching is best carried out in the classroom or by the specialist teacher.

What can I do to Help?

There is no one better placed to help a child with dyslexia than a willing and informed parent. Parents can help by understanding the difficulty, explaining it to the child, acting as an advocate for the child, informing teachers and other relevant people about the difficulty, maintaining the child's self-esteem, setting the difficulty in perspective and providing support for the child socially and educationally.

Are there Special Glasses for Dyslexia?

No. However, some people with dyslexia find it hard to read printed material when there is a glare from the page, so tinted or coloured lenses or tinted overlays have been found to reduce this glare and make reading easier.

What is the Difference between Learning Support, Resource, Remedial and Special Needs Teachers?

Learning support teaching is provided to children with low achievement. It was formerly called remedial teaching. It does not need an individual application. Assessment for access to such help is done in school through the use of standardised testing. The Learning Support Guidelines state that when selecting pupils for such help, priority should be given to those who achieve scores that are at or below the 10th percentile on a standardised test of English reading or mathematics.

Resource teaching is granted based on an individual application for a child with special educational needs to the SENO for the school. Such applications have to be accompanied by an assessment. At primary level children with dyslexia are considered higher incidence and so do not qualify for resource teaching. At second level the student has to be at or below the 2nd percentile in numeracy or literacy as well as having a specific learning difficulty.

Increasingly the term special needs teacher is being used, which describes both learning support and resource teaching.

What is the Difference between an IEP and IPLP?

Under the Education of Persons with SEN Act, an individual education plan (IEP) should be drawn up for the child who has been assessed as having special educational needs. For the child who falls within the criteria for learning support, an individual profile and learning programme (IPLP) is drawn up.

Each is very similar and records information about the learning attainments and learning strengths of the student. Both contain an outline of the learning programme that sets out learning targets and activities. There should be parental involvement in planning both.

Should my Child Continue in the Gael Scoil?

Research indicates that children with severe phonological deficits find it hard to cope with more than one language. However, every decision must be made with the individual child in mind and the advice of an appropriate educational specialist would be invaluable in such cases.

How does my Child get an Exemption from Studying Irish?

Children who have a specific learning difficulty and severe reading and spelling difficulties that place them at or below the 10th percentile on a recognised standardised test may be exempted from the study of Irish. Parents must write to the school principal, enclosing a report from a psychologist that is less than two years old. This report must specify the child's reading score and recommend the exemption (see Chapter 4). It should be noted that this situation is under review at the time of going to press.

If my Child gives up Irish, will this Limit Choice of Jobs or Universities?

Formal certificates of exemption are recognised by the National University of Ireland and so students holding such certificates will be exempt from college matriculation requirements in relation to Irish. The other universities and colleges do not have a compulsory Irish requirement. Irish is still required for training as a national teacher, some Civil Service occupations and a minimum of a grade 'C' in Foundation level Irish at Leaving Certificate is currently required for entry to the Gardaí.

What Help is Available for Students in Exams?

The Department of Education and Science offers reasonable accommodations in Junior and Leaving Certificate exams to students whose performance is impaired by their dyslexia. Students may be allowed the use of a reader to read questions correctly and/or a tape recorder on which to record answers, the use of a word processor or they may be given a waiver from having marks deducted for spelling and grammar errors. Specific extra time for students with dyslexia is not normally awarded (see Chapter 4).

Universities and third-level colleges offer a wide variety of supports in examinations and are very receptive to applications for such help from students.

Are there Special Computers for Dyslexia?

No, but there are many software packages that make organising and producing written work much easier (see Chapter 12).

Can I Get any Help with Expenses?

There is no doubt that providing support for students with dyslexia can be very costly. Parents are not entitled to any allowances, though schools may apply for grants for assistive technology for specific students. The cost of psycho-educational assessment is a valid claim on the Med 1 Form for taxpayers. Many parents have been allowed to claim tax relief for the cost of extra tuition. VAT can be claimed back on the purchase of computers/assistive technology for home/personal use via Form VAT 61A.

Why Don't Children Get More Help in School?

Unfortunately it is not possible for all children with dyslexia to get all of the help they need within the school system. Many parents find themselves looking for extra help outside of school. This may be because of limited resources within the school or because the child's problem is not seen as severe enough to warrant learning support. At present, dyslexia is regarded by the Department of Education and Science as a high incidence special educational need. This means that it is a difficulty shared by many pupils. Pupils with high incidence difficulties are not eligible for individual resource teaching at primary level. They are eligible to receive help from the special needs teacher.

16. Conclusion

Dyslexia is a complex condition. It is as old as mankind, but it presents as a problem only at a particular point in time. In pre-literate societies it would have gone unnoticed. While writing first appeared over 5,000 years ago, it was the preserve of a few. In any case, as early scripts were ideograms or picture scripts, people with dyslexia would not have had much difficulty either in reading or writing them. It is only within the last one hundred years that universal literacy has been the objective in the developed world. Interestingly, dyslexia as a phenomenon did not arouse much attention before the turn of the 19th century. In the future, information technology may well make reading and spelling less necessary. Being born in the 20th century was really bad luck for many people with dyslexia, because literacy has never been so necessary for education and for the workplace.

Many people with dyslexia say, and many experts in the area would agree, that dyslexia is not so much a learning difficulty, as a teaching disability. Because people with dyslexia learn differently, and because it is a minority way of learning, it is not well understood by teachers and is not catered for within mainstream schools. Many older people will remember when writing with the left hand was strictly forbidden in Irish schools – it was a minority activity and severely discouraged. Luckily this era has passed and hopefully in the future pupils with dyslexia will be accommodated as comfortably within schools as are left-handed pupils now.

What is needed to bring this transformation about? Greater awareness, greater acceptance and greater adaptability are required. Parents, teachers and education authorities need to acknowledge that dyslexia is a common condition affecting up to 10 per cent of the population and that even at the milder end of the condition the child with dyslexia has special educational needs. Increased awareness resulting in early identification and appropriate intervention is likely to yield significant results. The existence of dyslexia must be accepted and this means that dyslexia-friendly teaching must be provided and dyslexia-friendly schools must be promoted as an intrinsic part of the education system, not an optional extra when funds permit. The necessity of adapting to social and cultural differences is becoming apparent in our schools. Pupils with dyslexia may well benefit from this acceptance of diversity. Insisting that there is only one way of thinking, one way of perceiving the world, one answer to every question is a luxury that the Irish education system can no longer afford.

A growing economy needs all the help it can get. The talents and abilities of people with dyslexia can be harnessed. Their creative, visuo-spatial, problem-solving and inter-personal skills are assets too valuable to ignore. Literacy is the foundation stone on which education, academic success and qualifications are built. Society has little room for those who do not acquire written knowledge and the certification to prove it. As we do not yet have the means to bypass the literacy requirement, there is no choice but to alter our education system to meet the needs of learners with dyslexia, so that they also can access the knowledge that is acquired through the written word.

It is hoped that this book will help to bring that change about and that readers will find in it some of the information and encouragement they need. The authors wish all people with dyslexia and their families success in overcoming the obstacles that learning differently puts in their path, and the strength and determination to pursue that path and achieve their goals.

Appendix A:
The Dyslexia Association
of Ireland

The Dyslexia Association of Ireland (DAI) is a company, limited by guarantee, that has charity status. It was founded in 1972 by two women who had observed similar learning difficulties in their children. They had discovered that, though the children were bright and interested in learning, neither could read nor spell properly. Nobody seemed to know why this was, so they did some research. Having discovered that dyslexia was the cause of their children's difficulties, they set up an organisation to promote awareness of dyslexia and to lobby for the provision of state services for those affected by it. However, they also realised that children with dyslexia needed specific help and they needed it right away. Therefore, the DAI set about providing the information, psycho-educational assessment and specialist teaching that was needed. It is still doing so today, with more demand than ever for its services.

Information

The first, and often the most crucial, need of parents whose children are having learning difficulties is for information. The Dyslexia Association provides a public information service through a telephone helpline, an information booklet and a website (www.dyslexia.ie). Members of the association are kept up to date with developments through newsletters, public meetings and conferences. Courses for parents, talks to parent/teacher groups and in-service courses for teachers are also offered.

Psycho-Educational Assessment

Many parents who are unable to secure assessment for their children through the National Educational Psychological Service come to the Dyslexia Association. The DAI has been carrying out such assessments for over thirty years and provides a service for children and adults. Funding from the Further Education Section of the Department of Education and Science allows the association to offer subsidised assessment to adults with limited means. The cost of psycho-educational assessment is €350 (2005). Waiting lists tend to be long for both children and adults.

Branches: Almost Nationwide

The Dyslexia Association now has branches all around the country. Branches are run by voluntary committees of parents and teachers. They act as local parent support groups and lobbyists; they raise awareness and provide information. They also organise workshops, which provide supplementary teaching by trained local teachers.

Group Tuition

One of the earliest innovations of the association, and one of the most successful, is the provision of group tuition for children between the ages of seven and seventeen, outside of school hours. Special classes are offered for students at Junior Certificate and Leaving Certificate level. The teaching is done by specifically trained teachers and the pupil–teacher ratio is kept very low. Children must have been assessed as dyslexic before enrolment. Classes are usually held for two hours each week in a local school. These classes, called workshops, organised by voluntary branch committees, are available in almost forty locations around the country. Details of workshops can be found on the association's website.

Individual Tuition

The association maintains a list of teachers who have taken a course on dyslexia and who are willing to offer one-to-one tuition. Parents and/or individuals with dyslexia may access names on this list by becoming members of the association. Individuals must have been assessed by a psychologist as having dyslexia and a copy of a written report must be available before tuition can commence. Tuition is usually carried out in the tutor's home. Teachers are available in most parts of the country.

Course for Adults

A full-time course for unemployed adults with dyslexia is sponsored by the Dyslexia Association and administered by FAS. This course, which is the only one of its kind in the country, is located in Celbridge, Co. Kildare. Details are available on the DAI website.

In-Service Courses for Teachers

In-service courses for qualified teachers are offered at weekends, evenings and during summer holidays. Full information is available on the website.

Parents' Courses and Talks

Short courses for parents on how to help and support their children are organised and speakers are available to give talks to parent/teacher groups, employers and others.

Membership

Membership of DAI is open to any interested person. An annual membership fee is charged. See website for details.

For further information on the DAI, contact 01 6790276 or look up the website (www.dyslexia.ie). An information booklet is available by sending €2 and a SAE to DAI, 1 Suffolk Street, Dublin 2

Appendix B:
Useful Resources

Government Publications

Report of the Task Force on Dyslexia (2001)
The Education Act (1998)
The Education of Persons with Special Educational Needs Act (2004)
Understanding Dyslexia (2005) video, CD ROM, DVD
Learning Support Guidelines (2000)

Useful Books

Bartlett, D. and Moody, S. (2000) *Dyslexia in the Workplace,* London: Whurr.
Cottrell, S. (1999) *The Study Skills Handbook*, London: MacMillan.
Culligan, B. (1997) *Improving Children's Spelling, A Guide for Teachers and Parents*, Dublin: Elo Press.
Frank, R. (2002) *The Secret Life of the Dyslexic Child*, London: Rodale.
Hornsby, B. (1988) *Overcoming Dyslexia*, London: MacDonald Optima.
Mackay, N. and Tresman, S. (2005) *Achieving Dyslexia Friendly Schools*, 5th edn., Oxford: Information Press and BDA.
McCormack, W. (2002) *Lost for Words, Dyslexia at Second Level*, 2nd edn, Dublin: Tower Press.
Miles, T.R. and Gilroy, D. (1986) *Dyslexia at College*, London: Methuen.
Ott, P. (1997) *How to Detect and Manage Dyslexia*, Oxford: Heinemann.
Payne, T. and Turner, E. (1998) *Dyslexia: A Parents' Guide and Teachers' Guide*, North Somerset: Multilingual Matters Ltd.
Peer, L. (2000) *Winning with Dyslexia, a Guide for Secondary Schools*, London: BDA.
Peer, L. and Reid, G. (eds) (2001) *Successful Inclusion in the Secondary School*, London: BDA.
Reid, G. and Fawcett, A. (eds) (2004) *Dyslexia in Context*, London: Whurr.

Websites

Organisations

www.ahead.ie	Association for Higher Education Access and Disability
www.bda-dyslexia.org.uk	British Dyslexia Association
www.becta.org.uk	British Educational Communications and Technology Agency
www.cao.ie	Central Applications Office with links to the Higher Education Institutions websites
www.dyslexia.ie	Dyslexia Association of Ireland
www.education.ie	Department of Education & Science
www.nala.ie	National Adult Literacy Agency
www.ncge.ie	National Centre for Guidance in Education
www.ncte.ie	National Council for Technology in Education
www.nln.ie	National Learning Network
www.scoilnet.ie	Primary and post-primary school site
www.psihq.ie	Psychological Society of Ireland
www.sess.ie	Special Education Support Service

Study skills websites

www.learnforsuccess.info	Study skills
www.skoool.ie	Subject notes and lots more

Educational Suppliers for Learning Materials

The Early Learning Centre: Branches currently in Dublin, Galway, Limerick and Waterford.

ETC Consult, 17 Leeson Park, Dublin 6, Tel: 01 4972067.

LDA, Duke Street, Wisbech, Cambridgeshire PE13 2AE, England, Website: www.ldalearning.com.

Prim-Ed, Bosheen, New Ross, Co. Wexford, Tel: 051 440075, Website: www.prim-ed.com.

Stephens, Rosa, 52 Nutley Avenue, Dublin 4, Tel: 01 2698799 (agent for Dorling Kindersley, Barrington Stokes and other educational publishers).

Surgisales Teaching Aids, 252 Harold's Cross Road, Dublin 6W, Tel: 01 4966688.

Appendix C:
Acronyms

ADD	Attention Deficit Disorder
ADHD	Attention Deficit Hyperactivity Disorder
AHEAD	Association for Higher Education Access and Disability
CAO	Central Applications Office
DAI	Dyslexia Association of Ireland
DCD	Developmental Co-ordination Disorder
DEST	Dyslexia Early Screening Test
DST	Dyslexia Screening Test
FAS	Foras Aiseanna Saothair
FETAC	Further Educational and Training Awards Council
IEP	Individual Education Plan
IPLP	Individual Pupil Learning Profile
LCA	Leaving Certificate Applied
LCV	Leaving Certificate Vocational Programme
NALA	National Adult Literacy Agency
NCCA	National Council for Curriculum and Assessment
NCGE	National Centre for Guidance in Education
NCSE	National Council for Special Education
NEPS	National Educational Psychological Service
NLN	National Learning Network
NUI	National University of Ireland
PLC	Post-Leaving Certificate course
RACE	Reasonable Accommodation in Examinations
SENO	Special Educational Needs Organiser
SESS	Special Education Support Service
SLD	Specific Learning Difficulties
SLI	Specific Language Impairment
WISC	Wechsler Intelligence Scale for Children

Appendix D:
Glossary of Terms

Accommodations: Procedures and materials that allow individuals with dyslexia to complete school or work tasks with greater ease and effectiveness given their specific learning difficulties. Examples include providing a tape recorder, a reader or extra time in a written examination.

Alphabetic principle: Understanding that spoken words consist of sequential sounds and that letters in written words represent those phonemes.

Asperger's Syndrome: Often referred to as *High Functioning Autism*, Asperger's Syndrome is characterised by low ability to empathise and form reciprocal relationships, repetitive patterns of behaviour and intense absorption in special interests. Persons with Asperger's Syndrome often have extraordinary memories for facts. No delay in language or intellectual development occurs.

Assistive technology: Any device or system that helps to improve the functional capacity of people with disabilities. Examples include voice-recognition and screen-reading software.

Attainment test: A standardised measure of achievement in a particular skill or subject.

Attention deficit: Abnormal difficulty in concentrating or applying one's mind to a task for an acceptable length of time. The cause may be emotional or physiological. It may also be referred to as *short attention span*.

Attention Deficit Disorder (ADD): A condition thought to be neurobiological and genetic, whereby the person has more than usual difficulty maintaining attention for any length of time, is highly distractible, disorganised, forgetful and has difficulty taking in instructions.

Attention Deficit Hyperactivity Disorder (ADHD): A condition similar to ADD with the additional features of restlessness, overactivity and impulsivity.

Auditory discrimination in reading (sound discrimination): The ability to hear similarities and differences and process the individual sounds in words. Difficulty can lead to errors in auditory word attack, spelling by sound and in receiving information given orally, such as directions or dictation.

Auditory processing: In reading and spelling, this entails receiving, examining, weighing, understanding, ordering and remembering the constituent sounds of phonemes or syllables in words. A basic deficiency may involve a difficulty in retaining accurately in memory the order in which phonemes are perceived, i.e. auditory sequential memory. It may also apply to deficiencies in the speech process.

Dyspraxia/Developmental Co-ordination Disorder (DCD): A condition whereby the individual has more than usual difficulty with co-ordination, with organising movement and also has significant visual perceptual difficulties.

Blending (auditory or sound blending, auditory or sound synthesis): The process of combining or blending together two or more sounds or phonemes represented by letters to pronounce or spell words. In blending, each phoneme (sound) is represented by a corresponding grapheme (letter).

British Ability Scales (BAS): An intelligence test consisting of a range of subtests that measures intellectual ability. It is sometimes used by psychologists as an alternative to the WISC or parts of it may be used to measure specific functions such as memory.

Cognition: The process or processes by which an organism gains knowledge or becomes aware of events or objects in its environment and uses that knowledge for comprehension and problem solving.

Cognitive deficit: A perceptual/conceptual difficulty that affects intellectual functioning.

Consonant blend: Two or more consonants sequenced together within a syllable that flow together and are at the beginning or end of words, for example, bred, jump.

Consonant-vowel-consonant sequence (cvc): A pattern of three letters (e.g. c-a-t) or sounds (e.g. /s/-/a/-/ck/) that represent one of the most common sequences in English.

Content word: Any word with meaning such as a noun or verb.

Decoding: Changing letters into phonemes/sounds and blending them together to form words.

Differentiation: The process by which curriculum objectives, teaching methods, resources and learning activities are planned to cater for the needs of all pupils, including those with dyslexia. Differentiation is necessary to identify and meet the needs of each individual pupil within the classroom, especially those with learning difficulties.

Digraph: There are two types of digraph:

1. Consonant digraph – a combination of two adjacent consonants that represent a single speech sound (for example *gn* as in gnat, *th* as in thumb, *sh* as in ship, *ph* as in phone);
2. Vowel digraph – a combination of two adjacent vowels that represent a single long vowel sound (for example *ee* as in meet, *eu* as in euro, *oo* as in moon).

Diphthong: A vowel speech sound or phoneme made by gliding (through a change of tongue position) one vowel phoneme into another in a syllable (for example *o* glided into *i* in *oi* as in boil, or *o* glided into *u* in *ou* as in crouch). Note that each of the two consecutive vowels contributes to the diphthong's sound. The true diphthongs are: *au, aw, oi, oy, ou* and *ow*.

Dyslexia: A continuum of specific learning difficulties manifested by problems in acquiring one or more basic skills (reading, spelling, writing, numbers), such problems being unexpected in relation to other abilities.

Encoding: The techniques required to spell word parts and then whole words by breaking syllables into sounds and matching them to appropriate letters.

Function word: A word that does not have lexical meaning but primarily serves to express a grammatical relationship (for example of, or, and, the).

General learning difficulties: The term usually describes intellectual functioning where the person finds all aspects of learning difficult. A person with general learning difficulties will have been assessed as being in the Exceptionally Low range of intellectual ability on an IQ test (scoring below 70 on such a test). General learning difficulties are categorised as mild, moderate and severe. The difficulties extend to general functioning and are not specific to any one area of learning. An IQ score between 70 and 79 is usually described as 'borderline mild general learning difficulty'.

Grapheme: The smallest, single unit of a written language (i.e. a letter).

Inclusion: The process of providing services to students with disabilities in local mainstream schools in age-appropriate general education classes with the necessary support services and supplementary aids for pupil and teacher.

Individual education plan (IEP): A programme designed to address the individual educational needs of a student who is usually in receipt of supplementary teaching. An IEP should specify long-term and short-term learning targets and provide an indication of how those targets might be achieved.

Individual profile and learning programme (IPLP): An individual programme prepared for each pupil who has been selected for additional help in school. Like the IEP, it summarises the outcomes of diagnostic assessment and indicates medium-term learning targets related to the pupil's needs, and learning activities for school and home that are designed to meet these needs. It involves the pupil's class teacher, special needs teacher and parents.

Information and communications technology (ICT): The hardware, software and infrastructure used for the creation, processing and communication of information, as well as applications of that technology such as email and the world wide web.

Kinaesthetic: Movement of the body involving large or small muscle groups.

Learned helplessness: This refers to the tendency of some pupils to be passive learners that depend on others for decisions and guidance. In individuals with dyslexia, continued struggle and failure can heighten this lack of self-confidence and lead to learned helplessness.

Learning support teacher: Learning support teaching is provided to children with low achievement. It was formerly called remedial teaching. Assessment for access to such help is done in school through the use of standardised testing. The Learning Support Guidelines state that when selecting pupils for such help, priority should be given to those who achieve scores that are at or below the 10th percentile on a standardised test of English reading or mathematics.

Letter combination: A group of letters which, when combined, make a sound that is different from the expected blend of their individual sounds, for example *ing, ang, ung, ong, eng, ink, ank, unk, onk, tion, sion* and *ture.*

Lexical: Refers to the words or the vocabulary of a language.

Long-term memory: The final phase of memory in which information storage may last from hours to a lifetime.

Metacognitive learning: Instructional approaches emphasising self-awareness of how one learns such as memory and attention.

Mixed/crossed laterality (cerebral dominance): The tendency to perform some motor acts (eye, ear, hand, foot) with a right preference and others with a left.

Morpheme: The smallest, single unit of meaningful language. All words are morphemes.

Multisensory learning: An instructional approach that uses a combination of several learning channels or modalities, i.e. auditory, visual and tactile-kinaesthetic, in one learning-based activity. An example is tracing a sandpaper letter while saying the letter name aloud.

Non-phonetic words: Words that do not conform to the expected letter-sound correspondences of English. Examples include irregularly spelled words such as *laugh, yacht, Wednesday.*

Non-word: A phonetically-regular, pronounceable string of letters with no meaning – in other words, a nonsense word such as *gud, somp, shup.* A pupil's decoding (phonic) skills may be assessed by asking them to pronounce a set of non-words.

Orthographic awareness: Sensitivity to the structure of the writing system such as spelling patterns.

Percentile: A value on a scale of 100 showing the percentage of the distribution that is equal to or below it. Many test results are now given as percentile scores. A person's score at the 35th percentile indicates that 34 per cent of his/her peers would receive a lower score and 64 per cent of them would receive a higher score.

Perception: The extraction of information from sensory stimulation.

Performance test: A test composed of tasks that call for non-verbal responses. Seven of the thirteen sub-tests of the WISC-III are performance tests.

Phoneme: The single smallest unit of spoken language. There are approximately 44 phonemes in English.

Phoneme awareness: The ability to segment oral words into their constituent phonemes. Phoneme awareness is an important pre-requisite for reading and spelling.

Phonically regular word: A word whose pronunciation may be accurately predicted from its spelling.

Phonics: An approach to the teaching of reading and spelling that stresses symbol–sound relationships, especially in beginning reading instruction.

Phonology: The study of speech sounds (phonemes) and their function in language. In English, there are approximately 44 phonemes. Written English uses 26 visual symbols or graphemes, commonly called letters.

Phonological awareness: A language skill that is critically important in learning to read. It is defined as an explicit self-awareness of the phonological structure of the words in one's spoken language. It involves the ability to notice, think about and manipulate the individual sounds or phonemes and syllables within words.

Resource teacher: Resource teaching is granted based on an individual application for a child with special educational needs to the SENO for the school. Such applications have to be accompanied by an assessment.

Short-term memory: That aspect of memory that only lasts briefly, has rapid input and output, is limited in capacity and depends directly on immediate information. Short-term memory enables a reader to keep visual and auditory information in mind long enough (or until there is enough material) for processing. An example is analysing a word for blending.

Sound (auditory) blending: A sound-combining skill based on the ability to blend individual sounds into recognised words.

Spatial orientation: Awareness of one's own position and movement in space, primarily from visual and kinaesthetic clues. Directionality depends on spatial orientation.

Specific Language Impairment (SLI): This describes a delay in the development of expressive language and delays in both receptive and expressive language that are not the result of intellectual disability, autism, hearing loss or another condition. Difficulties can occur at the level of phonics, meaning, syntax, fluency and appropriate usage.

Specific learning difficulties: A student's learning difficulties, such as those arising from dyslexia, that are specific to a particular area (or areas) of the curriculum such as reading. Such difficulties are unexpected in relation to the student's other abilities.

Special needs teacher: Increasingly the term special needs teacher is being used instead of learning support or resource teacher.

Speed of processing: The term usually refers to both psychomotor speed and mental speed. On the Wechsler Intelligence Scale two/three subtests measure processing speed and results are in the *Processing Speed Index*. Research has indicated that one of the features of dyslexia is a slower speed of processing both verbal and non-verbal information.

Stimulus: An environmental event capable of being detected by the senses. Examples include speech sounds and spoken and written words.

Syntax: The conventions and grammatical rules for assembling words into meaningful sentences.

Tactile: Having to do with the sense of touch as a learning channel. An example is finger tracing over a sandpaper letter.

Transposition: A type of reading or writing error involving a change in the sequence of two or more sounds or letters in a word or words in a sentence. Examples would include writing *desrcibe* for *describe* or saying *pashgetti* for *spaghetti*. Some errors appear like anagrams such as *breaded* for *bearded*.

Visual discrimination in reading: The ability to see similarities and differences and process the visually distinctive features of letters, words and phrases. Difficulty can lead to errors of letter or word identification and interfere with reading.

Visual motor co-ordination: The ability to co-ordinate what is visually perceived with finer body movement (eye–hand). Examples include tying laces and handwriting.

Visual processing: In the reading and writing process, it entails receiving, examining, weighing, understanding, ordering and remembering the constituent letters or syllables of words. A basic deficiency may involve a difficulty in retaining accurately in memory the order in which letters are perceived, i.e. visual sequential memory.

Wechsler intelligence scales (WPPSI, WISC, WAIS, WASI):
These are tests of intellectual ability most frequently used by psychologists. They were originally developed in the US under the direction of David Wechsler. The tests used in this country have been adapted for use in Britain and Northern Ireland. They are revised periodically according to the most up-to-date research. The WISC, for example, is now in its fourth edition. They measure a range of abilities, verbal and non-verbal:

- Wechsler Preschool and Primary Scale of Intelligence (WPPSI) tests at the earliest stage;
- Wechsler Intelligence Scale for Children (WISC) tests children of ages 6–16 years;
- Wechsler Adult Intelligence Scale (WAIS) tests adults;
- Weshsler Abbreviated Scale of Intellligence (WASI) is an abbreviated scale.

Wechsler tests of literacy, numeracy and language are also used by many psychologists. Results on these can be compared with results one might expect from a child's level of cognitive functioning, assessed on the WPPSI and WISC.

Appendix E:
References

Augur, J. (1981) 'Games and Activities for Parents and Children to Play', *Dyslexia Review Supplement*.

Augur, J. (1997) 'Early Indicators of Dyslexia', *The Dyslexia Handbook*, London: BDA.

Burgoine, E. and Wing, L. (1983) 'Identical Triplets with Asperger's Syndrome', *British Journal of Psychiatry*, Vol. 143, pp. 261-5.

Gardner, H. (1983) *Frames of Mind*, New York: Basic Books.

Hynd, G. (2002) 'Neurobiological Basis of Dyslexia: Implications for Diagnosing Subtypes of Dyslexia and ADHD', *Paper presented at Policy on Dyslexia conference, Uppsala University, Uppsala, Sweden 14-16 August 2002.*

Kaplan, B., Wilson, B.N., Dewey, D.M. and Crawford, S.G. (1998) 'Developmental Co-ordination Disorders: How Do you Define what it is and what it is not'? *Paper presented at the Novartis Foundation Meeting.*

Kaplan, B., Wilson, B.N., Dewey, D.M. and Crawford, S.G. (1998) 'DCD may not be a Discrete Disorder', *Human Movement Science*, Vol. 17, pp. 471-90, August.

Mc Loughlin, D., Fitzgibbon, G. and Young, V. (1994) *Adult Dyslexia*, London: Whurr.

Morris, B. (2002) 'Overcoming Dyslexia', *Fortune Magazine, May.*

Moser, C. (1999) *Improving Literacy and Numeracy: A Fresh Start*. The report of the Working Group chaired by Sir Claus Moser: Department of Education and Employment UK.

Orton, S.T. (1925) 'Word Blindness in School Children', *Archives of Neurological Psychiatry*, Vol. 14, No. 5, pp. 197-9.

Orton, S.T. (1926) 'Reading Disability', *Genetic Psychological Monographs*, Vol. 14, pp. 335-453.

Peer, L. and Reid, G. (2003) Dyslexia: *Successful Inclusion in the Secondary School*, London: David Fulton Publishers.

Portwood, M. (1999) *Developmental Dyspraxia*, London: David Fulton.

Pringle-Morgan, W. (1896) 'A Congenital Word Blindness', *British Medical Journal*, Vol. 2, p. 1378.

Richardson, A.J. (2002) *Dyslexia, Dyspraxia and ADHD: Can Nutrition Help?* Dyslexia Trust Fund (www.dyslexia.org.uk).

Scott, R. (2004) *Dyslexia and Counselling*, London: Whurr.

Snowling, M. (2004) 'Language Skills and Learning to Read: Literacy Outcomes for Children at Risk of Reading Difficulties', *Paper delivered at Dyslexia Association of Ireland Conference, Dublin City University, April 17th, 2004.*

Stein, J. (2001) 'The Magnocellular Theory of Developmental Dyslexia', *Dyslexia*, Vol. 7, pp. 12-36.

West, T.G. (1991) *In the Mind's Eye*, Buffalo, New York: Prometheus Books.

Index